Amy Koit

KIDS MONEY HABITS

Self published by Amy Koit.
Sydney, Australia

Editor	Stephen Lake
Interior design	Eva Gomiscek
Cover design	Bogdan Matei

Contents

Preface

Some people ask about my credentials to guide parents to be intentional about teaching their children about money. More specifically, they want to know if I'm a financial planner. I am not a financial planner. I am many other roles – a lawyer, an accountant, an educator, a writer – but the most important role I bring to what I do is being a mother to three young children.

Financial planners create ways of achieving goals, usually with longer time-frames, often years. This is done after obtaining a lot of information about the client – age, dependents, income, expenditure, assets, liabilities, financial knowledge, risk profile and a lot more. This is not possible in a book, and in any case I am not a financial planner.

Instead, I help parents in their financial parenting journey, with a plan to guide parents to be intentional about teaching their children about money. The goal is financially literate children. This is not something than be easily measured or something that has a specific time to achieve. In fact, financial literacy is a goal that really has no end because children will continue on their journey to become financially literate adults. Adult children may then seek the advice of a financial planner to achieve their financial and life goals.

Financial planning differs from parenting. Most financial planning skills have limited bearing on teaching young children about money. For example, would a six year old be interested in how much tax he has to pay when he earns money from chores?

Parents are the most qualified people to give their children financial training for two very good reasons – young children have a close relationship to the parents and the parents are available every day. Children naturally look to their parents for guidance in many parts of life, and learning about money is just one of many.

Parents know best how to teach their own children and financial parenting works best when left to the parents, with guidance when needed. Rather than being told what to do, all we need is some guidance from other parents who have gone through the same process and have given a lot of thought into what works and what doesn't.

We don't need to be a financial planner to cultivate good money habits in our young children. As parents, we already have the financial parenting qualifications to teach them about money.

The challenges of parenting

Parenting has always been challenging, but being a parent in the 21st century has its own unique challenges. Never before have we had a world that is so connected. The pervasiveness of the internet at home, work and life has made it more difficult for parents to monitor the information that our children receive. Social media has a large influence on our children's view of what is and is not acceptable. As marketers move into the online world, rules governing traditional advertising are no longer effective. The availability of easy credit allows more people to buy more of what they want now, without having to earn the money and save first.

Parenting young children is exhausting work. There are many competing priorities that parents must juggle when it comes to raising children. On the schooling front, there are priorities to teach our children to read, write and do mathematics. On the life skills front, we are striving to ensure we build our children's resilience, combat bullying and teach our children many social skills such as making friends, team work and taking turns. We are also constantly on the look-out for cyber-security issues.

With these competing priorities in raising young children, it is no wonder our children's financial literacy is not even on many parents' list of priorities. We simply don't have any more capacity to fit it in.

After reading this book, many parents will realise that our children's financial literacy doesn't have to be another item to add to our list of priorities. All we have to do is be intentional in teaching our children about money. This means having frequent money conversations as part of the family's conversations, knowing the purpose of such conversations and how each conversation fits into our children's overall financial literacy journey. This book provides the plan for parents to know where each conversation fits into our children's overall financial literacy picture – it is a step towards building our children's understanding about money.

There is no better time to start than today. Follow my journey on the Kids Money Habits website (www.kidsmoneyhabits.com). Better yet, share your journey with me. I want to leave you with a quote that has often reminded me of my vision and purpose in writing this book for you:

Train up a child in the way he should go;
And when he is old he will not depart from it
~ Proverbs 22:6

Raising financially literate children – one habit at a time.

Acknowledgements

First and foremost, I want to thank my family.

To my children – *Elisabeth, Richard, David*: without you, this book would not have been written. You embraced my ideas and allowed me to share your stories. This book was written for you guys, with much love.

To my husband – *Alaric*: life is sometimes crazy, especially when ideas are constantly changing! As always, you came along for the ride and went with the flow. I know you will always be my biggest fan in everything that I do.

Other significant people who have influenced, encouraged and supported me throughout the writing of this book:
Lisa McInnes-Smith, Derek Gehl, Steve McKnight, Cath Johnson, Carla Reddy, Victoria Flanagan and Helen Bouzas, Sharyn McCowen, my editorial team (Stephen Lake, Eva Gomiscek, Don Gillmore), all my friends at the Australian Martial Arts Academy, members of the Mustachian with Children Facebook Group, members of the Kids Money Habits Facebook Page, followers of Kids Money Habits website blog.

Introduction

When I left the corporate world and said that I wanted to teach financial literacy, inevitably I was told anecdotes about segments of the community lacking in financial literacy skills. Most, if not all, people in these segments are adults. Many are women who, due to circumstances beyond their control, are now managing their finances for the first time.

While there are many support and education services for adults in this situation, they are simply a band-aid solution, solving problems without eliminating the problem itself. This is why I want to focus on teaching children financial literacy. I believe that financial literacy taught from a very young age will eliminate or minimise many of the problems arising from a lack of financial literacy in adulthood.

A young child's biggest influence is his or her parents. If I try to teach anyone's children directly, it won't be effective because they will only see me as another teacher. But I can teach the children's parents. I can show parents how to effectively cultivate good money habits in their children.

The Australian Securities and Investments Commission is a Federal Government agency, Australia's corporate, markets and financial services regulator. In June 2003 ASIC released Consultation Paper 45 *Financial literacy in schools.* The paper found the 18 to 24 year old group to have the lowest level of financial literacy. That was 14 years ago. That group is now 32 to 38 years old … parents of the next generation. These parents may be unsure how to teach their own children good money habits simply because they were never taught any good money habits. This is also the group that grew up with the Internet being widely available and therefore never had the chance to learn from observing proper money transactions. Parents falling into this category will benefit the most from what I have to share.

Why I decided to write about teaching children financial literacy

When I became a parent, I did what many parents do. I searched the internet to learn the most effective way to teach my children how to read and to do mathematics. I spoke to many parents about what they are doing with their own children to teach literacy and numeracy. I learned to teach my children to read by starting with the alphabet. To teach numeracy I began with counting 1, 2, 3. When my children started school they were given worksheets to trace to develop their writing skills. After a lot of research, I noticed a gap in one very important life skill. There are almost no resources on how to teach our children financial literacy. Where do we start if we want to teach our children financial literacy?

Since the GFC in 2008, governments around the world have been keen to increase people's financial literacy. Governments know they can't interfere with family life, so they cannot mandate that parents teach their children financial literacy (it's already difficult enough convincing parents of the merits of immunisation). So governments turn to the only means available to educate children in financial literacy – formal education. Since 2003, governments have put more resources into ensuring schools teach financial literacy from a much younger age than has been the case prior to 2003.

In 2012 ASIC launched its *MoneySmart Teaching Program* to incorporate consumer and financial literacy within the Australian school curriculum. In an article in the *Curriculum Leadership Journal*, Peter Kell, then Commissioner for ASIC, wrote this.

'By using real-life contexts, *MoneySmart Teaching* gives students the opportunity to learn:

- How to manage their finances and plan for their needs and wants, now and into the future;
- The language of money, how to navigate the ever-changing consumer and financial landscape and where to go for assistance;
- The rights and responsibilities of consumers in modern society and the wider impact of everyday consumer and financial decisions; and
- How to develop a range of enterprising behaviours.'

The *MoneySmart Teaching Program* has been adopted by Australian schools to varying degrees. This is due to the nature of the Australian political system – while there is an appetite for teaching financial literacy at the Federal Government level, the same is not necessarily shared by the individual states and territories. Therefore, while the Federal Government may offer suggestions on how financial literacy should be taught, the Federal Government has no authority to order schools to teach financial literacy. Such authority comes from the state and territory governments, which include financial literacy as an optional rather than a compulsory topic in the school curriculum. It is therefore left to the individual schools to decide whether or not and to what extent financial literacy is included in each school's curriculum. It is also left to the individual schools to decide how to teach financial literacy. Some schools have adopted the Federal Government's *MoneySmart Teaching Program*, but many have not.

My children's school has not adopted the *MoneySmart Teaching Program*, but nevertheless the children are learning about money to some extent. This suggests that Australian primary school students are learning a little bit about money, though not to the extent that I would describe students as being financially literate.

This begs the question: If schools are already teaching children a little bit about money, why do parents need to get involved in teaching children much the same thing?

The reason is that a young child's biggest influence is his or her parents. Being taught about money at school is merely learning about money in the abstract. It is financial knowledge but it is not financial literacy. Financial literacy isn't simply about adding up money or working out how much change to get back. It's about using financial knowledge and judgement to make wise money decisions. This can only be developed by giving children as many opportunities as possible to experience financial decisions in real-life situations.

A student's competency in a school curriculum is determined by completing set tasks or tests. Unlike reading, writing and arithmetic, it's not possible to measure a child's competency in financial literacy this way. The foundation underlying true financial literacy is habits, the formation of which depends on a person's attitudes, beliefs and values about money. None of these can be measured and unfortunately what doesn't get measured doesn't get done. So if it's not possible to measure a student's competency in financial literacy, it isn't something that is taught in primary schools as a priority. Parents will continue to have a vital role in teaching their children financial literacy.

This book explores basic concepts about money and discusses common habits often associated with financial literacy. Concepts such as earning, saving and spending money are the basic stepping stones to a child's financial literacy. Just like starting with ABC and 123, financial literacy begins with learning about earning, saving and spending. These are the areas we focus on to begin cultivating our children's good money habits from a young age.

Financial literacy is not complete without exploring the concept of donating, budgeting and investing. These are topics that will be explored in another book once the foundations habits are established. For now, the focus is on developing and strengthening the children's foundation in understanding basic money concepts.
Financial literacy is a lifetime journey that begins with cultivating good money habits. There are no tests to work out if your child has passed or failed; there are no IQ tests to determine how 'successful' your child will be in the adult world. This is their journey that begins with your commitment.

Chapter 1
TEACH ABOUT MONEY

Introduction

I speak to many parents about children financial literacy and we all agree on one thing – children should be taught about money. Despite this agreement, many parents do not teach their children about money at all and of those who teach, very few do so intentionally. Given the number of other life skills we want to teach our children, with reading, writing and numeracy often at the top of our list of priorities, this is understandable. This book is not intended to add to a parent's list of priorities – we already have so many *competing* priorities.

The purpose of this book is to encourage parents to be *intentional* in teaching their children about money. This means that the money lessons we teach our children are all pieces of a bigger puzzle and we know exactly where those pieces fit and which piece is next. As long as we are intentional about our teaching, it doesn't matter where the teaching sits in our list of priorities because we know money lessons are still being taught.

This introductory chapter explores the common reasons for many parents not wanting to be intentional in teaching their children about money. The chapter addresses these reasons and explains why we *should* teach our children about money.

Common reasons for not teaching about money

Many parents view any talk about money as taboo, so they are reluctant to talk to their children about money. Common reasons given by parents for not wanting to teach their children about money include:

- We shouldn't burden children with adult problems.
- We were never taught about money and we turned out fine.
- We have made so many mistakes with money, we're not the best people to teach.
- We might get it wrong.

I explore each of these reasons next.

We shouldn't burden children with adult problems

We want our children to remain innocent for as long as possible, to lead a life as care-free as can be. Some parents believe that talking about money inevitably leads to talking about money problems:

unable to afford to buy certain things; paying bills; getting a loan, etc.

Whether we like it or not, our children will eventually be exposed to money problems. The scary thing is that exposure is coming thick and fast – it's happening at an earlier age and its effects are bigger and quicker than before. The internet and online money transfers contribute to this phenomenon. As much as we may wish our children to lead a worry-free life with money for as long as possible, we are better off equipping them with the ability to deal with money problems we know already exist. For example, we should teach children about saving money so that they understand the importance of this to be able to buy the things we need or pay the bills.

If you're afraid of bombarding young children with warnings about money for fear it may cause anxiety in some children, it's best to gradually teach money skills in a form that suits the child's mental development and other factors. As parents, we choose the type of conversations we have with our children. The topic of conversation depends on our children's maturity and understanding of the world. When your child is ready for more complex money discussions, you can start to introduce the so-called 'money problem' conversations. Sometimes your children will lead you to those discussions. Keep an open mind and talk to them about it.

I never fathomed why my son David (then six years old) would ever discuss bankruptcy with me. How did it happen? Well, while out on a walk one day, he casually commented that he wished we had bought all of our household electronics from Dick Smith. When I queried why, he replied this would have kept the company from going bankrupt. He must have overheard a conversation my husband and I had a few days earlier about the company being put into liquidation. For many adults, the topic of bankruptcy conjures feelings of sadness, anger, desperation, hopelessness and melancholy. In the adult world, bankruptcy is a money problem. But for my six year old, he didn't see it as a problem. He was simply curious.

> The same money conversation can either be an education or it can be a problem. We have the ability to control where we take the conversation.

When having money conversations with our children, we need to be mindful of our own values, attitudes and beliefs. The same money conversation can either be an education or it can be a problem. We have the ability to control where we take the conversation.

We can choose to expose our children to money matters (including money problems) within a safe and controlled environment or we can let them be exposed to it on their own, in a very dangerous environment in the immediate future.

We were never taught about money and we turned out fine

Many of us learned about money as we went along, usually when we received our first pay check from a part time job. Most of us turned out fine. But the fact that you're reading this book means you've probably realised that you want your children to learn about money differently to the way you learned about money. Maybe you've watched your children develop money habits that you are not happy with. Or perhaps you're worried about the outside influences on your children's attitudes towards money. Maybe you're going through or have come out of a financial mess and you don't want your children to go through the same. The reasons for reading this book don't matter. Regardless of any background, we can and should teach our children about money.

I wasn't taught about money, at least not intentionally, in the way I am now teaching my children. I was simply an observer in my parents' financial journey. I too grew up to be a financially responsible adult. But I grew up in a completely different time to my children. I grew up with children who didn't have much, so I didn't want for much. I grew up playing hop-scotch drawn with chalk on the pavement, playing marbles, skipping rope and tags. We spent our days outdoors at the playground and we didn't have 24/7 children's TV channels so I didn't get bombarded with commercials all the time. In hindsight and compared to today's childhood, I would say I lived in a predominantly media-free bubble.

> ... we can and should teach our children about money.

But my children don't. They now have a multitude of after-school activities to choose from, holiday camps to go to and a vast array of electronics – iPads, iPhones, iPods, Nintendos, Xboxes and multiple 24/7 children's-only channels. My children are constantly being bombarded with messages to spend. Some are so convincing that even I have fallen into the trap.

For example, the flavour today seems to be STEM activities, Science, Technology, Engineering, and Mathematics. Coding camps and lessons in robotics are popping up all over the place. Don't get me wrong, these are fantastic activities for children, but there are so many to choose from. I have seen advertisements for coding lessons on Scratch, Snap, Stencyl, Raspberry Pi, App building, Game making and others. These are accompanied by messages such as 'The internet is the future' or 'The earlier we get our children coding the more prepared they will be for the future' or 'Digital disruption – are you preparing your children?' No doubt there is a lot of truth in what is being said. But when I step back and pause for a minute, I recognise they have all the hallmarks of advertising and messages to convince us to buy, using our children's future as a fear factor.

With so many different STEM activities and lessons to choose from, I was getting confused and somewhat anxious about choosing the right one for my children. This is obviously the reaction the marketers intended. I sought an explanation of the different lessons from a friend who is a computer software engineer. This was when I realised the different lessons are simply different computer programs that teach children essentially the same skills – what computers are capable of doing, how computers think and how to solve problems using computer language. The different programs are simply there to cater for children's different learning styles and aptitude.

With so many different STEM activities and lessons to choose from, I was getting confused ...

Giving children an exposure to different sorts of money transactions allows them to better understand what money is capable of doing, how money is used, and making wise financial decisions. Children have different ways of learning , including learning about money. When we use different ways of teaching our children about money, we are simply catering to the children's different learning styles and aptitudes.

> ... I was reminded of how times have changed since I was a child.

While writing this book I was reminded of how times have changed since I was a child. I grew up to be a financially responsible adult because there were a lot of opportunities to observe good money habits.

Credit cards existed as early as 1950 with the origination of the Diner's Club in the USA. However, credit cards weren't available to most people until 1978. From then on, its use became widespread. I was a child of the 1980s and 1990s – best time ever, in my humble opinion. I observed many money transactions in the form of notes and coins. When I accompanied my parents to the shops, they always paid in notes and coins. When we had to catch a bus, we queued up and bought the tickets with our notes and coins. When we put petrol in our car, we'd pay with notes and coins. I never saw my parents use a credit card. I remember seeing the green American Express cardboard in the letterbox every so often when I collected the mail. But these were just toys for us to play with and I had no idea what American Express was. As far as I was concerned, the American Express cardboard was no different to the cardboard tags on clothes. I was much older (in my early 20s) when I understood American Express to be a credit card company. I'm not sure if my parents ever had an American Express credit card, but if they did, I never saw them use it, or any other credit cards for that matter.

I grew up in an era when there was less automation than today. On a daily basis I observed hard-working people earning money. I grew up in an earn-save-spend culture because the adults of that time didn't have ready access to credit. Borrowing wasn't an easy option and earning and saving was a necessity. In that culture, I learned that if I wanted to buy an item, I had to wait until I saved up enough. Even then I had to wait a bit longer until my parents were available to take me to the shops because internet shopping did not exist.

Since the late 1990s the availability of credit has increased significantly and since the turn of the millennia, internet shopping has become widely available. Children today cannot fathom a world where there is no credit to use and no internet shopping. "Just order it online" is a common phrase I hear these days.

The availability of credit and widespread use of the internet have transformed the save-spend culture into one that is spend-repay. Our children are growing up in this spend-repay culture and most have no idea what save-spend is all about.

Circumstances under which I cultivated my money habits simply don't exist naturally any more. Unless I find ways to teach, unless I create an environment to expose my children to these lessons, they will not get a chance to cultivate good habits with money. Thinking about my children's financial literacy also made me come to terms with my own values, attitudes and beliefs about money. There are many habits that I want to pass on to my children. But there are also many other habits that I only developed as an adult when I started to think more holistically about the power of money to do good and bad things. These later habits are ones that I want my children to learn at a much younger age than when I learned them.

It's a long process to unlearn bad habits and learn good ones – it's easier to start with good habits.

We have made so many mistakes with money

What we have termed mistakes with money is the realisation that the way we used our money previously is not the way we would like to use money today. Whether we call this a mistake, an unwise decision, a reflection or a lesson, the essence of this is simply that we have realised we want to change one aspect of our money habit.

There's a saying that 'hindsight is 20/20'. Hindsight is indeed a wonderful thing when our reflection confirms wise decisions, but it's not so wonderful when that reflection tells us the decision was unwise. It's usually easy to know the right thing to do after something has gone wrong. So it is with money – it is often with hindsight that we realise we've made unwise decisions with our money.

> We learn when we reflect on what we have done and admit to ourselves that there is a better way of doing it.

Recognising unwise decisions is a process of self-reflection. We learn when we reflect on what we have done and admit to ourselves that there is a better way of doing it. A better way of doing things doesn't make the old way wrong. It simply makes the new way an improvement of the old.

We learn a lot about our own attitudes, values and beliefs about money when we are brave enough to ask ourselves tough questions and are honest with ourselves when answering the questions. For example, we need to ask ourselves why we buy what we buy. Is it to keep up with our friends? Is it peer pressure? Were we influenced by advertising? When we have spent a large sum of money, we need to be honest with ourselves and ask if we have done enough research on the item. Have we shopped around to be satisfied that the price we paid was a good price? Did the item we bought serve the purpose we originally wanted or did we give in to the bells and whistles for 'just a few extra dollars'?

In hindsight, many unwise decisions are essentially regrets. In hindsight, we regret that we spent so much money on buying lunch every day when it was cheaper to bring a packed lunch from home. In hindsight, we regret going out to coffee with friends every week instead of inviting our friends to our home for the coffee. In hindsight, we regret catching the bus to places when it was within walking distance. In hindsight, we regret paying so much for a fancy car when all we needed was something reliable to transport us from one location to another.

As you can see from the above examples, unwise decisions don't always involve large sums of money requiring lots of research. A few dollars here and there can add up to unwise decisions if it forms a bad habit.

Parents who regret the way they have used their money are in an ideal situation to teach their children how to reflect on unwise decisions with money. We should be able to explain to our children:

- What we did;
- Why is it unwise;
- When we realised it was an unwise use of money;
- What we have learned from that experience; and
- What will we do differently next time.

Having conversations with children about our money regrets can be very empowering for a child because she appreciates that even her parents can make unwise decisions with money. It is also very empowering for the parents because by talking about our unwise decisions, we own up to it. By explaining it to someone else, we begin a process of self-reflection. We start to question our attitudes about money and we either conclude that it is what we want to pass onto our children or we conclude that it is an attitude that stops with us.

Having conversations with children about our money regrets can be very empowering for a child because she appreciates that even her parents can make unwise decisions with money.

We might get it wrong

The fear of getting it wrong is one of the biggest barriers to many parents not having money conversations with their children.

Our attitudes will undoubtedly influence our money conversations with our children. So it's important that we acknowledge and recognise our attitudes toward money and work out whether we are comfortable with our attitudes.

If you want to pass on your good money attitudes to your children, then talking about money from your point of view can never be wrong. It is as good a start as any to your children's money education. If you are uncomfortable with your attitudes toward money, it is also a good start. This is the perfect opportunity for you to acknowledge your existing attitudes towards money and to explain to your children why they are not ones to adopt. This acknowledgement is a very powerful lesson. The most exciting part of this conversation is the journey you're both going to have as you both discover and develop new attitudes about money.

> ... I realised that the time 'when this can be afforded' never really arrives.

There is no right or wrong in your values, attitudes and beliefs about money. It is simply your own. The question is whether it is the same values, attitudes and beliefs that you want to pass onto your children.

It's useful here to give a personal example of a long-held belief, but one which I do not wish to pass onto my children. I have long held the belief that I would donate to charity when this can be afforded. As an adult, I realised that the time 'when this can be afforded' never really arrives. There is always a competing priority for my money – spending on the children, more entertainment, better quality food, redecorating the home, etc. As I reflect on my beliefs about donating, I decided that I want my children to incorporate charity as part of their daily lives, as part of their budget and as part of their weekly decisions about money. I don't want my children to reach a day 'when this can be afforded' to then learn about giving. So I changed the way I view charity. I started to make donations a part of my budget and started conversations with my children about fund-raising and making weekly offerings to our church. I talk to them about the different types of charitable organisations and how their donated money is used by the organisation.

Why we should teach children about money

The same could be asked of reading, writing and arithmetic. Why indeed do we need to teach our children to read, write and do maths? These are basic life skills that we all need in a developed society. When financial transactions were relatively simple and visible, financial literacy wasn't seen as a life skill to be taught – it was simply something that was observed and undertaken. But in a world where financial transactions are becoming increasingly complex and invisible, children need to be taught financial literacy as another basic life skill. By learning about the origins of money, its history and how it has been used for good and bad, children will have a deeper understanding of the concept of money. They will grasp that it is not simply something that we use to buy stuff. Money is inherently more powerful than that. Children will come to understand the psychology and mindset of having money and spending money.

... children need to be taught financial literacy as another basic life skill.

Money is used to buy many things: lollies, children's bicycle, school books, a night out, a car, a house, and a crib for the new baby. Knowing about money is important and it's equally important for parents to teach their children about the power of money, and the responsibility that should come with power. Sadly, history has shown that as some people and entities acquire more money, the responsibilities that ought to come with this power have not always been present.

Over time, many people have grown weary of the GFC (Greed for Cash) and watch with helplessness as generation upon generation abuse the power of money. We watch a child's carelessness with money in dismay and wonder how on earth generations of children have come to value so little.

Too many people attribute minimal or low value to many things. In the past, consumer items lasted for a long time. Today, too many consumer items are designed to last a short time, to be thrown away and replaced. Children are growing up in this throw-away environment. Fuelling this rate of consumption is the increasing availability of credit. Notice it is not money in the form of notes and coins that are available. It is the derivatives of money – loans and various forms of credit – that are increasingly available. Using the derivatives of money has consequences, one of which is the delay in time and space for the day of reckoning – the day the loans and credits have to be repaid with real money. Some people only see the consequence of having to pay interest on the credit they use. They don't see the bigger amount that must be repaid eventually – the original amount borrowed and a much higher interest amount. Sometimes the total amount to be repaid is more than double the original amount borrowed. All of it has to be repaid eventually. Isn't it easier to save up the original amount than to pay more than double the original amount?

Children are growing up in this throw-away environment.

I believe one of the reasons people attribute minimal or low value to things is because these things are no longer bought with money. Money is valuable and when we buy things with money, those things become valuable also. Loans and credits on the other hand do not have the same level of intrinsic value as money. In part, this is because the relatively minimal time and effort we put into obtaining these loans and credits is not commensurate with the large amounts of credit that is then made available to us. Add to this the idea that we have a long time to repay the borrowed amount and the result is we don't put much value on the amount of credit available. When we buy many things on credit rather than with money, those things lose their value from the buyer's perspective because those things were not exchanged from something valuable – real money.

> We don't realise how much we have actually spent until the credit card bill arrives later.

Another reason is the effect of using credit itself. Money is tangible and when we use money to buy things, the transaction feels real. We see the notes and coins that once bulged out of our wallets slowly being used up. We see a depletion of our hard-earned money. On the other hand, buying things on credit is an invisible transaction. The psychological and mental effects of seeing our notes and coins deplete with each transaction is not present when we use credit. We don't realise how much we have actually spent until the credit card bill arrives later. By then it's too late to change our mind about buying. The more frequently we buy on credit, the more we become acclimatised to having a debt. Prior to credit cards in the mid-1970s, debts for consumer items were generally unacceptable. Today, many things are bought on credit.

This is not to say that everyone who uses credit to buy things do not value their things. In fact, there are some things that are usually bought with credit, like the family home. I have found that people who value things despite being bought on credit are people who understand credit as simply using someone else's money and it's not a decision to be made lightly. They appreciate that there is a high cost to using other people's money and to minimise those costs, borrowed money must be repaid in the shortest possible time. The urgency of repayment collapses the time delay between using credit and the day of reckoning.

When children understand that money is valuable because they have exchanged their time, skills and effort for it, they begin to appreciate that throwing away things unnecessarily is no different to throwing away their money and this in turn, is no different to throwing away their time, skills and effort. In the long run, children will come to understand that buying things that last a long time is a better use of their money than buying things that are made to be thrown away and replaced. Perhaps our children will be the ones who will reverse the throw-away culture of consumerism – this is one of my hopes.

> Young children are the most teachable group ...

Because of the sheer power of money and the effects it can have on the mental health of so many people, it is important for everyone to learn about money, starting from the grass roots. A child's developing brain must be taught the effects of money so that they can fully grasp its power when they deal with larger sums of money later in life. Young children are the most teachable group because they do not have preconceived ideas of how life should be and are ready to absorb any lessons we wish to give them. This is why this book is written for parents of young children. We all have the ability to make a difference in our children's future financial literacy. It starts immediately.

Cultivating good money habits

While socio-economic status is often hereditary, it is possible to change with the correct mindset and attitude. Many post-war immigrants have amassed their fortunes through sheer hard work and determination, through frugality and saving and through carefully managing whatever money they have.

> ... we must begin with cultivating their good habits with money today.

Many parents today are aghast at the way their children spend money on things they do not seem to value. We worry that our children will grow up to become adults who do not have good money habits and will not know how to cultivate good money habits in their own children.

Many of our decisions involving money are the result of habits we developed throughout our life. To shape the way we use and manage money, we must begin with the habits we cultivate around money transactions. It is the same for young children. To shape the way we want our children to use and manage their money we must begin with cultivating their good habits with money today.

Children today are often not given the opportunity to cultivate good money habits. The environments in which they are growing up do not readily lend themselves to teaching good money habits. When we commit to teach our children good money habits, we find ways and manufacture circumstances to allow our children to practise good money habits. We create an environment for our children to practise good habits in a world that is full of bad habits.

Financial resilience and wisdom

The process of cultivating good money habits changes the way a child sees money. Their deeper understanding of what money really is and what makes it valuable changes a child's attitude towards the use of money and the things they exchange for their money.

Children who have not cultivated good money habits simply observe transactions happening with money, with no deeper understanding of what is really happening. Cultivating good money habits in children isn't simply going through money transactions in life and taking the child along to observe. It cannot be executed on auto pilot because we don't know what images our children are observing and we don't know what messages they are absorbing. If we want them to retain the good messages, we must be proactive in pointing out these messages to the children.

Money conversation: free money from the ATM
When my son David was five years old, he once asked me if we can buy his favourite treats. I said 'No' and explained that I didn't bring enough money to buy anything beyond what was on the shopping list. Of course he didn't know this was a deliberate decision on my part, so that we didn't spend unnecessarily on things we don't need. He then asked, 'Why don't you just go and get some money out from the machine at the wall?' I replied that I don't have any money to get out from the machine. This was the truth, as I had less than $20 in my account and the lowest denomination to withdraw from the ATM is $20. He replied, "That's why you go to the machine. It gives out free money!' That was the perfect opportunity for me to explain exactly what an ATM is and where the money *really* comes from.

There are many conflicting messages in the world of money.

Conservative, older approach	Riskier, modern approach
Except for a house and car, you shouldn't borrow money.	Debt for anything is fine. This is what credit cards are for.
Don't spend all your money, save some.	There's no point working hard and earning lots of money if you don't spend it along the way.
Work more or smarter to earn more so you can buy what you want.	Don't spend all your time working. You should enjoy every day of your life because you don't know what will happen tomorrow.
If you get into debt at a young age, you'll be bound for life.	If you don't have money to buy what you want now, it's okay to borrow because you can always pay it back later.

Children who have cultivated good money habits have an in-built resilience and wisdom to know what they want to do with their money. Despite all the noise out there, they are able to sift through the conflicting messages and ultimately make informed and wise decisions for themselves. In short, cultivating good money habits in children builds financial resilience and wisdom.

... they are able to sift through the conflicting messages and ultimately make informed and wise decisions for themselves.

If you don't teach them, someone else will

Many parents believe their children should learn money skills from the age of six years old, but believe it is not their responsibility to teach the children.

If parents aren't having money conversations with their children, someone else will fill that gap. Whether we like it or not, our children will be exposed to conversations about money. If it's not exposure from responsible adults, it will be exposure from a less ideal teacher: the media, or their equally clueless peers.

Marketing, through various forms of media, has always been about exploiting people's insecurities about 'not enough'. Not good looking enough, not thin enough, not smart enough, not spend enough money on children, not spend enough time with family, etc. Convincing us to give in and buy solutions to overcome these insecurities is the success of marketing.

Convincing us to give in and buy solutions to overcome these insecurities is the success of marketing.

Marketing that is targeted towards children is no different. It plays on children's desires to have more toys, more sound, more light, more gadgets, the latest craze, etc. Wanting more than what they already have is basically children giving into the fear of not having enough.

Billions of dollars are spent on advertising every year. Children are bombarded with advertising telling them how to spend their money. In her book, *This Little Kiddy Went to Market*, Sharon Beder writes that most children between the ages of two and five cannot

differentiate between television and reality because the critical, logical and rational mind is not yet fully developed. Prior to 12 years of age, most children do not fully understand that advertisements are trying to sell them something. Marketers are aware of this and produce advertisements to exploit this distorted reality.
Here are some more interesting facts from *This Little Kiddy*:

- In the US, food and drink companies spend $12 billion a year advertising to children and youths.
- Fast food outlets spend $3 billion on television advertising to children.
- Australian children see 12 television advertisements an hour – that's one advertisement every five minutes!
- The Teenie Beanie baby is believed to have sold 100 million Happy Meals in 10 days compared to normal sales of 10 million in a week.

> ... our children are being targeted by clever marketing.

If this is the only source of information children are getting, it will be the only lesson they learn. Social media fuels the list of influencers. To a large extent, social media is basically the rest of the world telling us what to spend our money on so we are accepted by society.

Whether we like it or not, our children are being targeted by clever marketing. They will need guidance from us if they are to overcome the tactics designed to exploit their vulnerability. Limiting young children's exposure to marketing in their formative years is a very effective way of ensuring that they are not learning bad habits before they are mature enough to learn the good habits. Young children are very trusting in nature. They do not question the correctness or accuracy of what they are told or taught. They simply believe everything is true. Learning to distinguish between marketing hype and facts is part of a child's journey in financial literacy. However, these cognitive skills are developed over time, as a child's thinking matures. In the meantime, it's important that children are not exposed to skewed messages before they are mature enough to develop and sharpen their critical thinking skills.

When my children were very young they did not watch much television. In part it's because they spent most of their days at daycare. In part, it was because as parents, we decided very early on that our children would not spend much of their time watching television. My husband and I also limited how much television we watched so the children were not indirectly exposed to advertisements. By the time my children were old enough to notice what their peers had, my children were already on the path to cultivating good money habits, including wise spending decisions. They did not succumb to the latest fads and craze from the school yard because they simply couldn't understand why people would pay a higher price for a particular branded item when a cheaper version has the same functionality. It also helped that they didn't recognise many of the popular brands because of their limited exposure to marketing.

As your children begin to sharpen their critical thinking skills, it would be a good time to explain to them the purpose of advertising. Perhaps have some fun with the advertisements. Annie Leonard, the brain behind the *Story of Stuff*, used to play a game with her daughter to see who can first identify the hidden message in each advertisement. Another parent would mute the television during commercial breaks and make up his own commentary about the product being advertised.

We have a choice: teach our children about money or let the media (or their equally clueless peers) teach them.

Teachable moments or skewed lessons

Our young children are the masters of the pester power. For those yet to experience it, I'm sure you have witnessed it in the shops. It goes something like this: a child sees something they want, often conveniently placed at their eye level. The child begs her parent to buy it. Parent either ignores the begging or says 'No'. The tantrum begins. What do the parents do?

> ... teach our children about money or let the media (or their equally clueless peers) teach them.

We know the correct answer and we can chorus what parents *should* do. This includes distracting the child with something else, threatening to withhold treats if they don't start behaving or ignoring them. Sometimes it's all of the above. But knowing what *should* be done doesn't always serve us well when we're the actors in the scene. We feel embarrassed, ashamed, angry, frustrated. Many of us (including me) have simply given in to the tantrum and bought the item.

In these situations, the media has won. The child has learned the lesson that they can have whatever they see and money is to be spent on whatever they want if they are persistent enough. They have not learned the other side of the coin – in order to have money to spend on whatever they want, money must be earned first. Even when we have earned the money, there needs to be a priority of things we need or want to buy. These are in fact teachable moments that parents can use to teach the children about the influence of media. The teachable moment doesn't have to be before we buy the item. It doesn't have to be in the middle of a tantrum. In fact, even if we end up giving in and buying the item for the child, this in itself is a teachable moment. It is an opportunity to explain to the child the effects of marketing and in this instance the media has won over both parent *and* child. In this instance, it was an unwise spending decision.

> If we don't use opportunities like these to teach children about money, they will learn only the skewed version of money.

If we don't use opportunities like these to teach children about money, they will learn only the skewed version of money.

Be intentional in teaching about money

We wouldn't neglect basic skills such as reading, writing and arithmetic. So why would we neglect teaching about money? As parents we often ask our children about their day. Who did they play with? What did they do at school today? What books are they reading in class? What is one plus one?

When we are intentional in teaching our children about money, the list of daily questions we ask our children should also include questions such as: Guess how much your lunch cost today? Guess how much we saved by walking to school today? Want to know what you did that saved us money today?

These money conversations are not taking place in many households because today's parents are busy and our children are over-scheduled. We are busy transporting our children from one activity to another and for families with more than one child it becomes a logistic and time management nightmare. I know this first-hand. My three children have various extra-curricular activities. It's not FOMO (fear of missing out) – the children are genuinely enthusiastic about all of their activities. But despite this busyness, many parents still find the time to ask their children about their day, so why not slip in a money question as part of this conversation? There are still plenty of opportunities to talk in the midst of all this busyness: there's the time in the car when we're driving to places; meal times; down times where we just do nothing (we talk or play board games instead of watching TV) and there are also those times when we get to the venue early and are waiting for the activities to start.

... many parents still find the time to ask their children about their day, so why not slip in a money question as part of this conversation?

Reading, writing and arithmetic are important life skills. It's time financial literacy is given the same importance, and taught to our children.

First a student, then a teacher

If we are to embrace the privilege of teaching our children good money habits and be a good teacher, we must first learn as a student – with an open mind. This may be extremely difficult for some adults who have preconceived ideas about money, based on what they have experienced and what they have been taught. But if we are to truly impart money lessons to a child, we must be willing to question our existing perceptions about money. We must begin to see money through different lenses – the good and bad things money can do; the unwise decisions we have made with money; the willingness to change our preconceptions about money and the courage to try new ways of teaching children about money. We don't know where our teacher will come from – sometimes it's other adults, sometimes it's ourselves but more often than not, it is our own children and their enquiring minds.

Before we can teach our children the values, attitudes and beliefs about money, we must first understand our own. We must recognise and accept our emotional response to transactions involving money, whether the reaction is positive or negative. If we don't fully understand and accept our values, attitudes and beliefs about money, we often become very defensive when our children start to question the money lessons we teach.

Adult attitudes and behaviour matter

More is caught than taught. Children pick up on their parents' habits so we want to be sure we are modelling what we want our children to learn. It may mean changing our old habits. Very often, if we ask our children to help us unlearn an old habit and learn new ones, children are quick to remind us when we slip up.

Money conversation: stop buying that cup of coffee!

I have a bad habit of buying a cup of coffee whenever I'm out and about. While saving for a camping trip, I declared that I will no longer buy my cup of coffee and each time I forgo that cup of coffee, I will add the money to the camping jar. But I can't resist the aroma of coffee beans in the morning. When I am

> tempted to buy a cup of coffee, my children are quick to jump in to remind me about the camping trip. If that doesn't stop me, they are also quick to remind me that they had to forgo things they wanted in order to save up for the camping trip. The latter is all I need to be reminded of the role that I am modelling.

Read the questions below and answer them. No one will read your answer or judge you so be honest. Your answers will reveal a lot about your own values, attitudes and beliefs about money.

How do you feel when the subject of money comes up?

- Do you feel indifferent, scared, uncomfortable, excited, enthusiastic, angry?
- Do you wish someone would quickly change the topic?
- Do you always make a joke out of it?

How do you feel when you see other people overtly display their wealth?

- Do you feel inspired, disgusted, ashamed, angry, happy, indifferent?
- Do you scorn at other people's display of wealth?
- Do you compare your wealth with that of others?
- Do you find out where other families go on holiday so you can tell a more glamorous story of your family's holiday?
- How do you feel about people who can afford to buy things you can't afford?
- How do you feel about people who can't afford to buy things you can afford?
- Do you complain about how much you perceive people spend or don't spend?
- Do you talk about how big or small your home is compared to other people's home?

How do you feel when you read about successful people?

- Do you think they were lucky to be born into a smart or rich family?
- Do you think they were at the right place and at the right time?
- Do you lament that you wish you could be that successful?
- Do you aspire to become one of them?
- Do you find faults with them – surely they cheated or lied to get to where they are?

Do you mostly complain about money matters?

- Do you complain about how expensive everything is these days?
- Do you complain about the number of charities that thrust a bucket at you every time you walk down the street?
- Do you complain about how children waste so much money?
- Do you prioritise work above everything else? (be honest!)
- Do you see interruptions as a welcome distraction or an irritation?
- Do you often say 'Just a minute while I get this done' or 'Maybe later' or 'I'll be there as soon as …'?
- When you're idle with your time, do you find yourself thinking about work?

Children will pick up and adopt our values, attitudes and beliefs. If you don't want them to grow up with some of these, then make the change in yourself first. We must first reflect and be honest about our values, attitudes and beliefs if we are to cultivate good money habits in our own children.

Summary

Many parents know that children should be more financially literate, but don't know who should teach them about money. Parents look to schools to teach and schools look to the parents to teach. Much of what we do involves money, so we should all be teaching the children about money – parents, schools, the community and government. Otherwise, our children will learn from a more undesirable source – the media or their equally clueless peers.

To be really literate in finance is a lifetime journey. The more children are exposed to how money works and learning about finance the more equipped they will be to continue the journey on their own when they are adults. Our intentional teachings about money when our children are young will be the stepping stone to their future understanding about money.

Chapter 2
MONEY BASICS

Introduction

For many children today, money is the plastic card they see adults use to pay for things. For some children, money is the notes and coins that people use to buy things.

To truly understand money and its value, it's important that children are familiar with the origins of money. Bonnie Worth's book *One Cent, Two Cents, Old Cent, New Cent* (based on the works of Dr Seuss) is a great read for children of all ages to learn about the evolution of money.

This chapter explores the concept of money – how do we define money? Is it valuable? How does it derive its value? The chapter explains how to start teaching our children about money, beginning with identifying the children's natural tendencies.

What is money?

One of the earliest archaeological evidence of a medium of exchange is sea shells; have this conversation with your children the next time you go to the beach! Over time, different things have been used as a medium of exchange: stones, gems, rare metals, gold bars, gold coins, coins made from other metals, coins with holes, and different shaped coins.

In its purest sense, historically, money is something that can be seen and touched and can be exchanged for something else. Coins and notes can be seen and touched and we exchange them for goods and services. This makes coins and notes real money. Many people also equate cheques, credit cards, loans, store cards, gift vouchers and coupons as money, but these aren't 'real' money. Using a credit card as an example, sure we can see a plastic card and we can touch it, but the card itself cannot be exchanged for goods and services. We use a credit card to allow someone else access to our coins and notes and the latter are then exchanged for the goods and services that we want. So apart from coins and notes, the other forms of 'money' are simply ways to access money – they are not money itself (no doubt this will change as we move into a cashless society).

It's easier for young children to understand money when there is tangible evidence of money. In the digital age of internet banking and online transfers, money has become more abstract than ever. We may like the convenience of online money transfers, but unless children are exposed to money in a more tangible way, their understanding of money and its ability to do things will be confused. To succeed in teaching our children about money transactions, we must find a way to bring the abstract into reality.

Bartering

The underlying basis of money evolved from the concept of bartering – the exchange of one person's item for someone else's item. Many children should be familiar with this concept because they have been doing this on many occasions, although they don't realise it.

A good example is trading food with each other at school at lunchtime. A scenario might be as follows:

George and Mary are having lunch at school and both seem to want something other than what they have in their lunch boxes. George has fruits in his lunch box and Mary has a packet of chips. George would like a packet of chips.

Unfortunately, Mary is interested in cupcakes and would gladly trade with George if he had the sweet delights she wanted. Since George didn't have cupcakes he would have to find a school friend who has cupcakes and barter them for his fruits. This would give him a chance to trade with Mary and finally have his packet of chips.

This type of bartering is a very inefficient and time consuming process. In our example, George will need to ask a lot of people and search for someone willing to give up their cupcake in exchange for his fruits.

He might get lucky and find someone with cupcakes who likes fruits. Or he might have to work harder if his friend, Stacey, has cupcakes but wants muesli bars. This time, George will have to find another friend, Harry, to exchange his fruits with Harry's muesli bars, then find Stacey to exchange the muesli bars for her cupcakes, then find Mary to exchange the cupcakes for the packet of chips. Not only does this take a long time, but by the time George finds Harry, Stacey and Mary, Mary might have already bartered her packet of chips with someone else.

Understanding the concept of bartering sets the foundation for children to understand the role money plays in today's society.

Medium of exchange

The next step is to explain to the children the concept that money is simply a medium of exchange. When we buy food, we are simply exchanging what we have (money) for what we want or need (food). Similarly, when we work to earn money, we are simply exchanging our time, skills and effort for money. This is similar to bartering, but unlike bartering, money is a more effective exchange medium because it is common: everyone can use it to exchange for something else.

> Understanding money as a medium of exchange will open a child up to possibilities of earning 'money' in forms other than the notes and coins ...

Understanding money as a medium of exchange will open a child up to possibilities of earning 'money' in forms other than the notes and coins that they have become accustomed to. Imagine explaining Bitcoin to a child! Reward charts and the various permutations of reward system that many parents, teachers and educators already adopt is using the same underlying concept as money. One difference between these rewards and money is that the former cannot be used to buy the things that the children need or want.

Value of money

This was a difficult concept for me to write about. In part, it was because of the stigma associated with viewing money as something valuable; and in part because it's difficult to explain.

In order to write about why money is valuable I had to understand why I value money and then overcome my own uneasy feeling about being perceived as money-hungry and Scrooge-like. But the more I reflected on this and the more I understand my own values, beliefs and attitudes about money, the more I came to accept that viewing money as a valuable commodity doesn't define me as a person. I am simply viewing money for what it is. The way I use money will more accurately define my values, attitudes and beliefs about money.

> ... viewing money as a valuable commodity doesn't define me as a person.

So what makes money valuable? I *know* money is valuable. But what is it about money that makes it valuable?

There are many factors that influence the value of money. It could be influenced by supply and demand for the money, or the underlying value of what the money symbolises, or the ability to do things with money. It doesn't matter which of these reasons I choose to explain to my children why money is valuable. The end message is still the same – money is valuable, for whatever reason they understand it. The reason(s) you choose to explain why money is valuable will largely depend on what your children have been exposed to and their level of financial maturity.

I explained the concept of value to my children by reference to scarcity. An item is scarce if it has a limited supply and there is a high demand for that item. Underlying the intrinsic value of an item is therefore its scarcity.

Many of the older generations learned scarcity from living through an economic depression or recession. Children of that older generation grew up observing scarcity because during times of economic depression or recession, many people were living in poverty and this was visible. Children of that older generation cultivated the habit of being resourceful in times of scarcity. Today, it is difficult for many children in middle- to upper-class families to understand economic scarcity because they do not witness poverty first-hand. Even families who are living below or near the poverty line today often try their best to hide this from their children.

Today, it is difficult for many children in middle- to upper-class families to understand economic scarcity because they do not witness poverty first-hand.

While we do not wish economic recession or depression on anyone or anywhere, if we are to teach our children the value of an item through the lens of scarcity, we must find a way to manufacture an environment of scarcity.

Value through scarcity

Is money scarce? I initially thought so. Most developed societies rely on money to buy food, pay for shelter and to pay for conveniences such as electricity, gas and water. We need it to pay for education, clothes and leisure activities. So there is no doubt money is in high demand. By my reasoning, the limited supply of money and a high demand for it ought to create scarcity in money. If money is scarce, then it must be something a lot of people want and be willing to work for.

> ... if money is scarce, why won't some people work even when they are paid?

My reasoning changed when I had a conversation with a friend one day. She complained that her children will not do any housework, despite her offer to pay them. She reasoned this is because the amount she pays doesn't buy much these days (incidentally, she pays double what I pay my own children to do housework).

This got me thinking: if money is scarce, why won't some people work even when they are paid? At the other end of the spectrum, why do some people work for free? There are people in the society who work *pro bono* and many more volunteer their time in the community. Don't these people need money? How is this possible, given the high demand for money?

Then it dawned on me. It is not money that is scarce. It is what was given up in exchange for the money that is scarce. When we are paid to work, we are exchanging our time, skills and efforts for money. The higher our skill level, the greater is the demand for our time, skills and efforts. The value of our time, skills and efforts are imputed onto money when we accept money in exchange. Some people work for no pay because they see their contribution in time, skill and effort equally as valuable as (if not more valuable than) the money they would otherwise contribute towards the cause(s) they support.

Money conversation: is money valuable?

One day, while hanging up the laundry, I decided to ask my son Richard (then eight years old) why money is valuable. I thought I might get a better insight into how children think about money by asking a child; sometimes children are the best teachers.

Me	Do you think money is valuable?
Richard	Yes.
Me	Why?
Richard	Because we need it.
Me	Why do we need it?
Richard	We need it to survive – like buy food and drinks and clothes.
Me	But animals survive and they don't need money.
Richard	But we need money to buy what humans need to survive.
Me	So if we have enough to buy what we need, does that mean any extra money is not valuable?
Richard	No. It's still valuable.
Me	Why?
Richard	Because we need to save it up to buy shelter. We need shelter.
Me	Okay, let's say we have enough to buy everything we need – food, clothes, shelter, anything else we need. And we still have extra. Is that extra money still valuable?

Richard	Yes.
Me	Why?
Richard	Because we can then buy what we want.
Me	So is money valuable because we can buy anything we want?
Richard	No, spending money that way is just wasting money.
Me	Why is it wasting money?
Richard	Because it's a waste of our effort.
Me	Tell me what you mean.
Richard	We put in effort and time to earn that money. To spend it on anything is just wasting our effort and wasting our time.
Me	So what do you think makes money valuable?
Richard	The things we can buy with it.
Me	Does this mean if we buy expensive stuff, then money is more valuable but if we buy cheap stuff, then money is not as valuable?
Richard	No. Money is money.
Me	So what do you think makes money valuable?
Richard	I can't really explain.

I noticed Richard's replies often refer to the use of money to buy what we want and need with money. But what we want and need is not always scarce, especially items coveted by young children. I had a light-bulb moment.

Me	Do you think it's valuable because it's the connector between what we need or want and how we get it?
Richard	Yeah. So the more things we want, the more money we need. And the more money we need, the more we need to work. The more we work, the more time and effort we use up.
Me	So what do you think makes money valuable?
Richard	The time and effort we put into earning that money.
Me	And why is time and effort valuable?
Richard	Because time is something you can never get back.

So this is my family's theory of what makes money valuable – there are two aspects of this:

- What was given up for the money; and
- Money being the connector between what we want and need and how we get it legally (assuming what we want and need can be bought with money).

By my family's theory, if my children refuse to complete their paid household chores, they are refusing for two reasons:

- They value their time in doing other more important things; or
- They do not need or want many things, therefore do not require the money.

When children understand the link between needing more money and therefore needing to work more, the next conversation becomes a very powerful one. We should ask: Is it *money* that we need?

If we really need money, how was it possible that civilisation has existed and thrived for so long without the modern day notes and coins? If we really need money, how is it possible for other creatures on earth such as cats, dogs, fish and other animals to survive?

When we get down to the details of what we really need, it is not money. It is food, shelter, conveniences, etc. that we need and that money pays for. The more things we need or want, the more we need money to pay for them.

> If a child understands that money is a medium of exchange, he will understand that it is not money we all need.

This conversation is really the precursor to conversations with our children about needs and wants. If a child understands that money is a medium of exchange, he will understand that it is not money we all need. What we really need is the thing that we exchange with our money. The fewer things we need, the less money we need and the less we need to work. In Chapter 7 the concept of needs and wants is discussed in more detail, as well as ways to identify whether an item is a need or a want.

Money and happiness

Does money make people happy? This is a tough question because it depends so much on how happiness is defined. And there are so many definitions of happiness!

The short and most obvious answer is that money does not necessarily make us happy. Many of us know of people who have lots of money but are quite obviously unhappy. But there are also people who have a lot of money and are also very happy. On the flipside, we all know of people who do not have much money but are very happy and also 'poor' people who are very unhappy.

> People with money also have the freedom to decide how to use their time ...

The closest to truthfully answering this question is that money itself doesn't make people happy – it is what people do with money that makes them happy.

Money gives people choices that are not otherwise available, but too many choices can lead to unhappiness. People with money have a choice to do activities or buy things that bring them joy or achieve their goals; they have the choice to outsource activities that doesn't bring them joy or hinders their goals. People with money also have the freedom to decide how to use their time – whether to work or pay someone else to do that work for them. Having the freedom to choose how we use our time will lead to more satisfaction in life than a life where other people dictate how our time is to be used.

Again, happiness and joy have different meanings for different people and no one can be in perpetual happiness all of the time.

As you become more intentional in teaching your children about money, there will be many instances where you will be able to have a conversation with your children about the effects of their purchases. These examples reinforce the underlying message that money itself doesn't bring happiness. It is what we do with money that matters.

How to teach children about money

As our children grow up they will inevitably go through troubled times. We encourage an open dialogue with our children about their friendship groups, what happens at school, bullying, sex, drugs, alcohol, etc because we want to equip our children to handle these situations. Many adults face money problems and yet many parents are not talking to their children about money to equip them to handle these problems.

We want our children to be comfortable to talk to us about money because money lessons are taught one conversation at a time. Having frequent money conversations with our children removes the taboo barrier of money. We then find ways to reinforce those conversations using various tools and ideas.

> ... money lessons are taught one conversation at a time.

The great thing about having frequent money conversations is that they will never end. There will always be opportunities in life to continue these conversations and it becomes more diverse and more interesting and more exciting to engage in conversations as your child's financial literacy matures.

Money conversations are not like other conversations that can take place at certain times. Unlike the question 'Where do babies come from?' money conversations must take place frequently. The nature of the conversation evolves as a child's understanding matures. Even though the transaction itself and the lessons may be the same, no two conversations are ever the same.

Understand your child's natural tendencies

I believe all children are born with a natural tendency to either save or spend. Some children's tendencies are yet to be revealed. This is certainly true with my children – one is a natural saver, another is a natural spender and a third is somewhere in the middle, whose tendency is yet to be revealed, though I suspect he's leaning towards a natural spender.

Understanding a child's natural tendency enable parents to tailor conversations according to what makes sense to the child. Conversations about the importance of saving money are unlikely likely to do much to inspire a natural saver whereas a conversation about the difference between saving and hoarding may interest him. Similarly, conversations on the importance of spending money will only justify a natural spender's spending habits whereas conversations about responsible spending is likely to have more effect on him.

I am unsure if a person's natural tendency can change over time. I was a natural saver, but I did go through a spending spree during my teenage years and early twenties when I started to earn more money. Now that I am older, I have gone back to being more comfortable as a natural saver. Perhaps my natural tendency changed over time. However, I have read that everyone has to go through a few years of crazy spending to get it out of their system before we buckle down and behave more responsibly with money. So maybe I have always been a natural saver, but the rebellious child in me had to prove that I could be a spender if I wanted to.

Before we even begin to have a money conversation with our child, it is important to work out the child's natural tendency. We will then be able to better tailor our money conversations to that tendency.

Money conversations with children

The only rule about talking to children about money is to be yourself. Children can sense when parents are not being genuine, so be honest with yourself and with your children about your own values, attitudes and beliefs. We may not always like our values, attitudes and beliefs about money, but being honest keeps it real for the children. As children learn and begin to develop their own set of values, attitudes and beliefs, they will often question ours. It's difficult not to get defensive about this, but it's important that we respect the children's questions and give them some thought. Remember our teacher can come from anywhere, especially the children.

We may not always like our values, attitudes and beliefs about money, but being honest keeps it real for the children.

Keep it light-hearted, natural and free-flowing. Anything else will sound like a lecture or a 'direct and dictate' session and they will resent having these conversations. Ask them questions about what they are thinking and be interested in their answers. This will give you an insight into your child's thought process. It will tell you a lot about your child's personality and tendencies. Some children are natural savers, some are natural spenders. Some over-indulge and some under-indulge. Some children like external rewards along the way to keep them motivated, while others remain focussed on their outcome regardless of rewards or obstacles. Learning about each child's personality allows you to tailor your strategies and communicate in ways to really get your message across to different children. Only you will know your child best – not the teacher, not the coach, not the supervisor. You know how to best engage your child.

Choose words carefully

Words are very powerful. If words are repeated often enough we start to believe them. With this in mind, the words we use when talking to young children is very important. We want to remain positive and affirm that the process of cultivating good money habits is part of the children's learning journey in financial literacy.

Take the word 'mistake'. The online English Oxford Living Dictionary (https://en.oxforddictionaries.com) defines 'mistake' in terms of 'misguided' and 'inaccurate'. These words suggest that a mistake is made when the best course of action was taken but the outcome turned out to be incorrect, unwise or undesirable. A 'wrong' on the other hand is defined by words such as 'unjust' and 'immoral'. A mistake is therefore the result of a course of action whereas a wrong is a state of being. Adults may understand the difference between a mistake and a wrong but many children will not have the sophistication to understand this subtlety.

Adults may understand the difference between a mistake and a wrong but many children will not have the sophistication to understand this subtlety.

Some people label unwise money decisions as mistakes. Many acknowledge that despite these mistakes, it was the best decision they could make with the given information at that time, in the prevailing circumstances. I think this works very well when communicating with adults because adults are able to move beyond their mistakes with money.

When I talk to young children about unwise money decisions, I try to avoid using the term 'mistake'. As a child I was a perfectionist. I didn't cope well with making mistakes. I wouldn't have a go for fear of making mistakes. I would not try new ways of doing things unless I was assured that the outcome was totally correct. To me, making a mistake was as good as being wrong. In fact, when I am told I have made a mistake, I think what I am doing is wrong. Recognising that some children have this perfectionist tendency and many will not understand the subtle difference between a mistake and a wrong has made me cautious in the words I use with young children.

> In their journey to achieve financial literacy, children will make many unwise decisions before they learn to make wise ones.

When it comes to money, I do not believe there is a universally accepted way of deciding what to do with it. For example, an observer may say that going shopping and buying lots of clothes with our hard-earned money is a mistake or even the wrong thing to do. But for the shopper, shopping may be his therapy from an otherwise difficult day at work. To the shopper, using his money to buy clothes to make him feel better isn't a mistake – it's therapeutic. So much of how money is used is tied to our own values, attitudes and beliefs about money. These are not attributes that can ever be correct or incorrect for the decision maker.

In their journey to achieve financial literacy, children will make many unwise decisions before they learn to make wise ones. If a perfectionist child is constantly told he is making mistakes with his money, he will begin to think his values, attitudes and beliefs about money is wrong. This will have a negative effect on his self-reflection, discovery and willingness to embrace new habits with money.

I prefer to explain money mistakes to children in terms of wise or unwise decisions. Wisdom comes with age and experience and young children lack both to make wise decisions. We expect young children to make many unwise decisions with their money before they learn to make wise ones. When we have this expectation of our children, our mindset is one of understanding rather than judgement whenever our children make unwise decisions with their money. We understand that financial wisdom is not a race; it's a marathon that ends only when we decide we no longer want to learn.

> Wisdom comes with age and experience and young children lack both to make wise decisions.

Our role as parents is to guide our children to reflect on their decisions with money, and in that process they begin to refine their own values, attitudes and beliefs about money to achieve financial wisdom.

Keep It Short and Simple (KISS)

Talking to children about money is different to speaking with an adult friend about money. With children, it is important to keep it appropriate to their developmental level.

For example, teaching a five year old about compound interest isn't going to be effective. Teaching a teenager about what each coin or note denomination looks like is also not effective.

For young children, the KISS principle is a good guideline – Keep It Short and Simple. Young children have a very short attention span – they're here one minute and the next minute they are off thinking about something else. When speaking with young children, keep in mind they don't have a sophisticated vocabulary nor do they have an attention span that allows you to explain the meaning of sophisticated words.

When discussing money concepts, it is the financial development stage of the child that is important, not their actual age in years. My six year old engaged me in a conversation about bankruptcy – I'm not sure how many six year olds understand what that word means!

It may be helpful to take yourself back to your child's stage of development and think about money in children's terms. For example, when young children ask a parent how much he or she earns, they are not likely to expect a number in reply. To a young child, $5 is no different to $50. What the child is really asking is why he can't have everything he wants and why he can't have that ice cream or packet of chips when everyone else is having one.

When speaking with young children, keep in mind they don't have a sophisticated vocabulary ...

I find it's easier not to take their questions personally when I remember the innocence of children's questions. Their innocence is also something to keep in mind when answering questions about sensitive matters: children are likely to repeat it to people outside the immediate family.

A common question children will ask is if you earn more than your neighbour or your child's teacher or whoever else they come in contact with. Be careful when answering such questions because you don't know to whom your child may repeat the answer. This is an opportune time to remind the children that it's not a good idea to compare them with other people because we don't really know the true state of the other people's finances, just like other people do not know the true state of our finances. Whether you earn more or less than someone else shouldn't matter because the real question is whether you earn enough for your needs. One person earning more money than someone else doesn't make that one person rich or the other person poor. Being rich or poor in a money sense does not depend on how much comes in, but how much is kept.

> It is an even bigger fallacy when we start comparing our worst with what we *perceive* to be other people's best.

Another common question I have been asked by all of my children is whether we are rich or poor. Again, the children do not mean to be rude – they simply want to know whether we fit into the category of 'rich' or 'poor'. This is where I explain the many definitions of 'rich' and 'poor'. Some people are rich in the money sense; some people are rich in the spiritual sense and others still are rich in the happiness and love sense. What is important is we reinforce the message that we should not compare ourselves with other people. We should not compare what we have with what other people have. Simply having more stuff doesn't make a person rich because that stuff might be borrowed or bought with a bank loan. It is an even bigger fallacy when we start comparing our worst with what we *perceive* to be other people's best.

Start a conversation

As with many of life's basic skills, the earlier we start a conversation about money the better. After all, there is no minimum age that marketers target. Everyone is a potential target, regardless of age – this includes babies! So the earlier we get in, the better it is for our children's financial future. In our daily lives, there are many teachable moments to begin a conversation with our children about money.

> The more you practise having money conversations, the easier it becomes.

To start with, pick one money lesson that you want to teach your child and give yourself a timeframe to start a conversation about this lesson. As you go through your daily activities, consciously look for transactions that lead to that lesson. You can pick the topic you want to discuss or you can be led by your child's interest. Then talk about it. Ask your children questions about what you see. Listen to their responses. Ask more questions and listen some more. There is no time limit in these conversations. Sometimes a conversation can be over in five minutes. Sometimes it can occur in short spurts but span a few days. Sometimes the same topic presents itself in different ways over a few days. You may choose to present the concept once and then leave it for a while, or you may wish to repeat the same concept until you get some feedback that the children understand the concept. The more you practise having money conversations, the easier it becomes. The more you look for teachable moments, the more these opportunities present themselves.

Topics to talk about

Anything! Everything we do is somehow tied to money. Even a simple task as brushing our teeth has many money lessons tied to it. The cost of water, usage cost (so don't keep the tap running!), cost of toothpaste, cost of toothbrush, the advertisements telling us to buy the different types of toothbrush and tongue brush, dental costs, etc. The list is endless.

There is a misconception that money talk is serious and boring. It doesn't have to be – it can be as serious or as light-hearted as we make it. Once my children understood where money really came from, when I use the credit card to make payments, I have often joked: 'This is free money that I'm using, right?' They wisely reply 'No' and I will have fun with them by playing devil's advocate to why credit card should be seen as free money and give them a run of their debating skills!

> Allow your children to make unwise decisions with their money.

Our aim is to get the children interested about money and to notice that everything they do leads back to money. When you're ready and when they are ready, you can begin the money lessons – how to use money, the effects money can have, etc.

Allow your children to make unwise decisions with their money. Their process of discovery is a money conversation in the making. Perhaps you've gone through that same process of discovery – that same unwise decision – but on a much larger scale. If so, tell the children about it. Perhaps you thought it was an unwise decision, but then things somehow worked out to be the better. Again, tell the children about it. Let the children learn from their and your unwise decisions. Let them know it's a process of discovering how to use money. Similarly, let them learn from your successes and reward their successes as well. This can only happen if you continue to have an open dialogue with the children about money. Your purpose is to guide, advise, encourage and praise.

There are many other life values that we can tie into our money lessons and money conversations. Some of these include:

- Nothing of value comes easily.
- Live differently today so that you can live differently in the future. When others spend, you save because you have a goal you want to achieve. When others are indulgent, continue to deny yourself because you want to get to your goal quicker.
- While other children are being indulged by their parents, your child is learning the importance of focus, strength and determination to reach their goal.
- The difference between hoarding and saving.
- Good decisions come from experience, and experience comes from bad decisions.

Include all family members

Money talk is not reserved for adults only and it is not reserved for children of a certain age group. The earlier a child is exposed to money talk, the earlier a child develops his financial acumen. In this regard, including younger siblings in money conversations with an older child is beneficial.

Some conversations need to be family conversations so that every member in the family is on the same page. Other conversations may need to be done one-on-one to teach the child concepts that are more appropriate to the child's development stage in more detail.

The following topics may be the subject of family conversations:

- Saving for family goals;
- Paying for the family's activities;
- Paying for groceries, school excursions and clothing;
- The family's values, attitudes and behaviour towards money;
- Explaining pocket money – what it is, why you're giving, how much, when it will end, rules of use; and
- The effects of advertising and how the family will respond to advertisements and peer pressure about buying things.

Family sessions are also an opportunity to show the children that parents have a list of things they want or want to do, but that parents also have to say 'No' to themselves if it's not in the budget. I have a list of things that I would like to buy, ranging from small items such as a blanket for the worm farm to big items such as a new carpet or kitchen renovation. From time to time, I show the children my list of things I would like to buy and explain why I can't have everything I want on the list.

There is no special skill involved in having a conversation with children about money. All it takes is for you to start talking!

A young child seeks guidance from those they admire and trust the most – their parents, guardians and carers. These people are in a privileged position to have the most profound impact on the child's development. It is a privilege that must not be taken lightly, and must be recognised and embraced as a gift. What will you do with this gift and privilege?

Summary

There are many things in life we are uncomfortable doing, but we know we ought to do them because they're good for us. Money is an uncomfortable topic of conversation for many of us, but we know it is one of the most important topics to discuss to improve our children's financial literacy.

As with many of life's uncomfortable-but-good-for-us things, the more we practise, the more comfortable we will feel. It's the same with money conversations. The more we talk about it, the more natural it feels and the more normal it will be as a topic of conversation within the family and elsewhere.

Intentionally teaching our children about money means being intentional with our conversations. Money conversations can and should be intentional and natural – all it takes is practise!

Chapter 3
EARNING

Introduction

'Sometimes I like being at school more than being at home because it's harder work at home' says Elisabeth, my 11 year old daughter. I winced when I heard her say that. I thought our home is a place of love, laughter, fun and safety.

When I dug deeper into her comments, it turned into a teachable moment with many money conversations that follow. I asked her what she meant by 'harder work at home' and she replied the chores and housework she has to do at home is harder work than school work. To dispel any questions, her brothers also have their share of household chores.

It is true my children work hard at their chores at home. It is the type of hard work they will not get to learn anywhere else until they get a job. When my children are gainfully employed, I want them to be working hard for their employer and contributing from the very beginning, rather than starting to learn about hard work. So the money they earn from doing hard work at home is a lesson I want my children to learn – earning money *is* hard work. Later on, I will be using this lesson to encourage my children to invest their money wisely so they don't have to work hard for too long in the future.

This chapter explores the underlying basis of what earning money entails and why it *should* be hard work.

What is earning?

Earning money is not the opposite of spending money. Earning money is also not simply 'money in'. At its core, earning money is the exchange of very valuable and finite resources for a medium of exchange. The very premise of 'earning' is the value of our own time, skills and effort. When we work to earn money, we are using our time, skills and effort to perform tasks in exchange for money. It is this exchange for money that characterises the activity as 'earning'. Doing the same thing without receiving any money in exchange is not earning money. We know our children have understood the concept of earning money when they understand that it involves performing tasks with their time, skills and effort in exchange for notes and coins.

Why we should teach children about earning

'People know the price of everything and the value of nothing.'
~ Oscar Wilde

A child who has to earn her dollar will understand the effort and hard work that goes into getting that dollar. She will appreciate it more than if she is simply given the dollar. Children will truly appreciate the value of money when they appreciate the concept of 'earning'.

Many parents, teachers and educators implement reward charts in the home, school and even childcare setting. When a child or student makes progress towards an outcome set by the parent, teacher or educator, the child gets rewarded with stamps, stickers, etc. These stamps or stickers may subsequently be exchanged for toys which the child brings home to show mum and dad. We praise the child for getting the stamps, stickers or toys because we recognise this is the reward for their hard work and progress. Yet when it comes to rewarding the child's hard work with money, we seem to disagree on its appropriateness.

There is a belief that asking our children to work for money is child labour. No, it's not! We teach our children many of life's basic skills – brush their teeth, get dressed, pour their own milk. What's wrong with teaching them to work, why people work and how to work? Teaching our children to earn money reinforces the idea that money is not available and given to us simply because we exist. To have money, we must first work for it and earn it.

Time is (not) money

There is a common saying that 'time is money'. On one level it's true. Anyone who has to pay for a lawyer, accountant, doctor or dentist will know that the longer we engage their professional services, the more we have to pay them.

But at its core, time is not money. It is more valuable than money. Whereas money can be printed, manipulated and borrowed, usable time only exists in the present. It cannot be bought, it cannot be manipulated and it certainly cannot be borrowed. Time waits for no person; it's finite and can never be replaced. We cannot ask for our time back and we cannot make more of it. No one has been able to travel back in time and no one has been able to stop time. When 24 hours is up, the day is gone.

Teaching children to appreciate time as a finite resource changes the way they think about using their time. They can either use their time to argue with each other or with mum and dad, throw a tantrum or whinge about unfairness in their life, or they use that time to do something useful.

> ... time is not money. It is more valuable than money.

Once a child sees the real value of time, we may wonder whether she will refuse to work to earn money. Given the minimal effort required to undertake leisure activities, wouldn't she prefer to play instead? After all, life's short, so she ought to enjoy it as best she can, right? Later in this chapter, I discuss a few ways we can encourage our children to earn money. It is useful to point out here that a child who is capable of this depth of thinking understands that her time is finite and she has a choice in how to use it. She also understands the difference in the effort required to perform leisure activities and the effort required to work. If left unguided, she is likely to refuse to work especially if the work doesn't earn that much money. When a child is capable of this depth of understanding, we must engage her further in the next level of money conversation.

> If left unguided, she is likely to refuse to work specially if the work doesn't earn that much money.

Here are some questions to ask your child to get the conversation going at a higher level:

1. How can we earn more money with a given amount of time?

If time is finite and valuable, how can we maximise the return for a given output of our time, skills and effort?

Say your child is earning money by delivering leaflets to letter-boxes. Whether your child delivers one leaflet or five leaflets, she must still walk the same route. Rather than deliver only for one company, can she source leaflets from multiple companies and deliver multiple leaflets at the same time? While there will be a small increase in time and effort, the extra income easily compensates for this.

Another example could be selling lemonade. Instead of selling just lemonade in that time, why not have other goodies (such as popcorn) for sale as well? These questions will start your child thinking about the efficiency of her own time. If she's refusing to work because of the low pay, this could be the spark to get her working again.

2. What is your motive for working? Is it only to earn more money? Or is there something else of value that warrants giving up your time?

This is the perfect opportunity to teach your child other non-monetary reasons people work. Most people work for money because money is what most people need. However, there are people who do unpaid work for other reasons:

- They want to contribute to society, for example volunteers or the stay-at-home parent;
- They value the experience it gives them to find a better job; and
- They value the opportunity to learn new skills or refine their existing skills.

> ... helping other people gives them a sense of love ...

In Chapter 7 I discuss Maslow's *Hierarchy of Needs* in more detail. For the purposes of this chapter it suffices to explain that according to this theory, a person's physiological and safety needs must first be satisfied before the person is able to do things for a higher order of reason, such as for love and belonging.

In developed countries, many young children's physiological and safety needs are readily satisfied. Children have plenty of air, food, water, shelter and clothes and they have the safety of their parents looking after them and nurturing them. It comes as no surprise that many young children are very generous in their outlook. Many are happy to help out even without getting any money in return because helping other people gives them a sense of love and belonging. Why not find ways for them to help around the home? While praise from parents helps to reinforce that reward, we must be careful not to over-praise the children if we wish to maintain this inner motivation over any external validation.

Children who grow up with the attitude of helping others will lead a more satisfied life, including as adults. In contrast, children who are brought up thinking the only reason they work is to earn money or to get their parents' praise will eventually become dissatisfied with their work, which can then lead to burn-out or depression. So while we should encourage our children to work to earn money, we should balance this by pointing out non-money reasons for working. A child who refuses to work for money reasons could be convinced with altruistic reasons.

It is also the perfect opportunity for us to reflect on why we work. This is a conversation in itself!

Children who grow up with the attitude of helping others will lead a more satisfied life ...

3. If you are not using the time to work, what else would you be doing? What is the value of the alternative activity?

If your child would have mindlessly watched TV or played on their various electronic devices, is this a better way of using their time than using the same time to earn money? Ask your child how she feels after watching TV or playing on her electronic devices for a long time. Then ask how she feels after helping mum or dad or her siblings with a difficult task. This will get her thinking that it's not just the time she has lost – she has also lost out on an altruistic feeling.

If your child is mature enough to understand Maslow's *Hierarchy of Needs*, perhaps ask her which of her needs are being satisfied by watching television, playing with toys and helping someone else.

Money isn't everything

Whilst it is important to teach our children to appreciate the value of earning money through hard work, it's equally important we teach children gratitude along the way. We remind our children to be grateful for parents who love them so much to teach them about money. Children who are paid to do chores should be grateful that their parents have money to pay them, and may not know that many children are simply expected to do chores without being paid.

Whilst it is important to teach our children to appreciate the value of earning money through hard work, it's equally important we teach children gratitude along the way.

My personal story

It was difficult for me to be definitive about the conversations we ought to have with our children about being employed outside the home. Not only are there laws to regulate how children are to be employed, it is also an area where our own values, beliefs and attitudes about children in employment are most important in deciding what lessons to teach to our children. My values, attitudes and beliefs will be different to yours and what I teach my children in this area may be very different to what you teach your children.

My values, attitudes and beliefs in this area are very much shaped by my own upbringing and experience. A personal story about the young me may help explain the position I have adopted and what I teach my own children.

From a very young age, I grew up wanting to earn my own money. I attribute this to reading books written by Enid Blyton, most notably stories about children completing chores for family and working for friends to earn money and save up for a special item or event. Though I understand the reasons now, when I was ten years old it frustrated me to no end that no one would employ a child.

Undeterred (sometimes ignorance is bliss), I would trawl the classifieds every weekend, looking for jobs that a child could do. My persistence paid off when I spotted an advertisement looking for walkers to do leaflet deliveries. (In some parts of the world this is called junk mail or catalogues.) I jumped at the opportunity and asked my older brother to ring up on my behalf. I figured being a girl and sounding childish wouldn't convince anyone that it would be safe to give me the job. So my brother made the phone call and I landed that gig. I shared the responsibility (and pay) with an older brother and a younger brother. I was so proud to be earning my own money when I was ten years old. I felt very grown-up and mature and very capable.

> I would trawl the classifieds every weekend, looking for jobs that a child could do.

Having the leaflet delivery gig didn't pay very much, especially after splitting the pay three ways. To maximise the pay, I continued to look for leaflet delivery opportunities from different companies. Over time, we added more companies and my brothers and I would walk the one route but deliver leaflets for multiple companies at the same time. When I was 11 years old, I had built a business 'empire' with a system in place.

Despite the multiple sources of leaflet income, the pay still wasn't that great. But I didn't care much for the pay, I was happy to be paid anything at all. To me, any money that I earned outside of the home was my own money, not money given to me by my parents. However, the other valuable lessons I learned from that first gig were more important than the amount of pay.

I learned a lot about being efficient with my time. I learned about having more than one source of income and maximising my time in earning money. I learned to delegate and how to convince other people to give me a chance. I learned to be strategic in the routes I took so that I didn't double up on the same street and I learned how to double-check stock quantity. Of course I didn't learn all of these on my own. Despite my mother being busy with her own work, she saw value in getting involved with helping her children. I learned a lot from observing how my mother organised things. For example, she would ask us to tie the folded leaflets up in bundles of 50. This was a way to double-check the number of leaflets the distributor had specified and paid us for. It was also a way to work out strategic drop-off points to restock our bags, as it was impossible to carry all the leaflets in one bag. On reflection many of my mother's actions could have gone unnoticed and unappreciated. This realisation was a reminder for me to have frequent money conversations with my children so that I am intentionally teaching them about money, rather than leaving it solely to their own observations.

> I learned a lot about being efficient with my time.

I will be forever grateful to Lyn for giving me the chance to deliver leaflets. Many parents don't want their children to perform such labour-intensive work and to many people, the pay rate for the time and effort that goes into delivering the leaflets isn't worthwhile. I agree it was a physically demanding work. But for me, the pay rate was irrelevant. If I wasn't outside delivering leaflets and earning money, I'd be at home being bored anyway. More than the money I was paid, it would become the turning point in my resolve that age is no barrier to doing many things. This mentality has served me very well later on, as I entered the professional workforce. In addition, I believe the physical demands of delivering leaflets made me appreciate the less labour-intensive jobs that I would subsequently have.

> ... age is no barrier to doing many things.

Attitude of gratitude

As my history shows, I learned gratitude from a very young age and it is gratitude that motivated me to work hard and work smart to deliver value in the various roles that I occupied throughout my career. Until this day, I continue to be grateful for everyone who have given me a chance and who have supported me along the way. I consider myself very fortunate to have come across so many kind people along the way.

I am teaching my children to be grateful when it comes to outside work. It's important that I have conversations with my children about gratitude for someone else's willingness to give them the opportunity. Someone is willing to take the risk and give them the experience; in most cases people are also willing to pay them for doing the work.

When my children are too young to be legally employed, if someone offers to pay them to do odd jobs here and there, they ought to be grateful for it, because legally, they can't get paid to work anywhere else. Unless they would otherwise be using that time wisely, being paid is a bonus: whatever work they are doing at that age is a new experience. When they are of legal age to be employed, I want my children to appreciate the opportunity and experience. The pay is an important aspect of a job, but the experience they get is invaluable and no amount of money can compensate for it. They should appreciate that opportunity and learn as much as they can, as early as possible, in whatever work that they do.

The pay is an important aspect of a job, but the experience they get is invaluable and no amount of money can compensate for it.

Money conversation: an attitude of gratitude

There's a canteen at the stadium where Elisabeth trained twice a week with her basketball team when she was ten years old. She often arrived at the stadium early and I suggested she offer to take coffee orders for the canteen. She was excited and pitched the idea to the canteen owner. The owner agreed that for every coffee order she took, she would be paid 50 cents commission. So twice a week for eight months that year, she would turn up to the stadium early and do her coffee rounds. The conversation I had with her at that time was one of gratitude – be grateful that the canteen owner agreed to let her take coffee orders and thereby developed her customer service and conversational skills. Also be grateful for the owner willing to pay her to take coffee orders.

My role is also to guide my children to walk the fine line between being given an opportunity and being exploited. As with many lessons, whether we see something as an opportunity or exploitation depends very much on our values, attitudes and beliefs. Whilst I saw my leaflet deliveries as an opportunity, the career counsellor at my university saw it as exploitation.

> ... a grateful child will do the best work she can, regardless of whether and how much she is paid.

We will never really know if a child is grateful, because gratitude is something that is intrinsic to a person. But a grateful child will do the best work she can, regardless of whether and how much she is paid. The grateful child will understand that it's not just about how much money she earns, it's about the skills she is developing and the appreciation that someone is willing to give them a chance and teach them the skills. The child will become proactive and take the initiative to ask to do extra work or extra shifts, more than what she is expected or taught to do because a proactive child knows that the more work she does, the more skills she will learn. A grateful child is also one who takes pleasure in doing her work well and completing her tasks to the best of her ability. She is someone who compliments more than she complains.

There is an intrinsic pride that comes with working. There is a sense of completion and a sense of accomplishment when a child fulfils their work responsibility. When we give small jobs to children to complete, we are also training them to take on bigger jobs later in life. If they cannot demonstrate their competence to complete small jobs, how can they be expected to get the bigger jobs done properly?

Ways to encourage children to earn

Be a persistent parent

When children are young, there usually isn't any resistance to working. Many young children like to be helpful and this should be encouraged with lots of praise. My youngest child, David, grew up watching his siblings do housework and started helping with housework as soon as his fingers were strong enough to peg and unpeg clothes (around the age of two to three years old). At the time of writing, David is seven years old and hasn't yet complained about completing the chores that are assigned to him. On the contrary, he still asks for additional jobs to be done around the home and often asks 'How can I help you today, Mummy?'

As children grow older, they will begin to complain about working. This is regardless of whether the child was brought up helping out around the home from a very young age. The only difference is that a child who wasn't expected to work at a young age complains louder and more frequently.

> As children grow older, they will begin to complain about working.

So what can we do when our children start complaining about doing their chores, regardless of whether they are being paid to do the chores? The same thing we would do when our children complain about doing their homework. There is debate as to whether homework is actually beneficial to children and studies have shown that whilst homework generally is not beneficial, reading a book every day improves a child's literacy skills compared to children who do not read every day. The use of the word 'homework' in this chapter is to describe the beneficial type of homework. What do we do when our child refuses to do her homework? We continue to encourage, persist and insist:

- First we explain the importance of homework. We may also explain the role homework plays in her overall education. Similarly, we would explain the role that they all play in the family and why chores must be done.
- We might then paint a picture of the future – if she gets into the habit of doing homework at a young age, she will be able to better plan her activities when she gets to high school. We can paint a similar picture with chores by explaining that if they do simple jobs well, they show mum and dad that they are capable of handling more responsibilities.
- Finally, if all else fails, we may impose consequences for not doing homework or chores. That is, no electronics time, no extra-curricular activities, no play dates, etc.

So the parenting skills we use to teach our children about money are no different to those we use to teach our children other life skills.

What do we do when our child refuses to do her homework?

Find opportunities

When children are young, they do not have much exposure to the world around them to find ways of earning money. In the early years, we might have to help them find opportunities and more importantly, have a conversation with the children about how we found these opportunities. Over time, these conversations will develop the children's ability to find their own opportunities in the future.

My children have various ways of earning money – inside the home and outside the home. At home, they are paid to do chores. I had explained to them the reasons they are paid for completing chores. One of my purposes of explaining the reasons was to provide the children with a guideline to help them identify other chores to add to the list of paid chores. If the children find other ways to help out around the home that fit within the criteria, they are encouraged to discuss the chores and negotiate a pay rate with me.

> ... with each business venture, they took on an increasingly active role in managing their business.

The first way my children earned money outside the home was selling lemonade. They didn't come up with the idea themselves, but they were very receptive to it when I first suggested it to them. In the summer months, they would visit our local playground after school and sell lemonade and popcorn to school children at the playground. Over time, with my help, they worked out the ideal pricing for a cup of lemonade and a bag of popcorn. They also figured out why some venues or some time periods were popular and why some weren't so popular. They had a lot of fun running this business, and repeated this over the next few years. In providing suggestions to the children when they were younger, I had indirectly cultivated their entrepreneurial spirit.

Their subsequent business ventures were also not entirely their own suggestion, but with each business venture, they took on an increasingly active role in managing their business.

Pay for completing household chores

One of the earliest and widely used methods to encourage children to earn money is paying children to do household chores. In addition to learning about 'earning', paying for completing chores also present many opportunities to teach children about other money concepts. For example, if a child completes her work quickly, you may wish to reward her efficiency with a bonus. Similarly, if a child has taken the initiative to do more work around the home (for example offering to wash your car) you may wish to reward the child with a bonus. This is also a great way to help your child achieve her saving goal without her knowing that you're helping her (especially if this is her first goal).

Young children are often eager to help and do any housework asked of them. They do not fully understand the varying difficulties of work. For young children, mowing the lawn is the same as feeding the family pet. Having a tiered system to reward the varying difficulties of work won't make much sense to young children. It works best if you set the same amount for each household chore. Keeping it simple is the key.

> Ask the children to list tasks they think they *can* do (rather than chores they are already doing).

Older children who understand the degrees of effort required to complete different chores around the home will want to be paid accordingly. One way of ensuring the pay is commensurate with the chore's level of difficulty is to list the chores to be done with its associated pay rate. You can involve the whole family in this conversation by asking the family to help formulate the list of chores. Ask the children to list tasks they think they *can* do (rather than chores they are already doing). Then ask the children to rank the chores in the order of difficulty from most difficult to easiest. It's up to you if you want to help them along by giving them the criteria of what you think makes a chore easy or difficult. I prefer to leave it to the children to work it out amongst themselves first and only step in if they start to argue over the criteria. You can then add to the list of housework that you wish to delegate to the children (I added washing out the lunch-boxes and wiping down shelves to our list when I got fed up with doing them). Make it clear that it is the parents who set the rate of pay for each chore listed.

Once you have the list of chores and the associated pay rate, older children can choose the chore they will do, knowing how much they will be paid for completing the chore. This is helpful for the child who is very keen to reach her saving goal – the higher pay rate will mean more difficult work, but the child will achieve the goal sooner. To ensure the same child doesn't pick all the easy chores all the time, have guidelines on how many times a chore can be completed by the same person in one month. Alternatively, rotate who gets first pick each week.

Find deals

Children have more time than their parents. We can utilise this time effectively by encouraging the children to identify savings for various bills around the home. For example, you could challenge your teenager to shop around to find the cheapest electricity plan for the home. Ask her to ring the various utility companies and ask for the deals available. Then ask her to present to you the different options and explain why her chosen option is the best deal. To reward her hard work, you could agree to either split the savings identified or simply give the whole savings to her.

Younger children can also participate in a similar exercise. Pick a few items from the shopping list and ask your child to find the best deal for those items over the next 2-3 weeks. You will have to help her get access to the various catalogues from the shops or teach her to read online catalogues for her to do a price comparison. Once she has identified the best option, either split the savings with her or let her keep the savings.

Keep them motivated

I'm a firm believer of goal setting. A goal gives purpose for what we do when the going gets tough. It's our 'why' – why are we doing what we do? When writing and publishing this book, there were many obstacles. Some days I thought it was easier to just abandon this writing project. My children will still continue their financial literacy journey at home and I will still continue to research, read and come up with new ideas. There is really no need to write a book about all of this. But then I go back to my goals. Why am I writing this book? I have three reasons for writing this book:

- To achieve a childhood dream of being published;
- To give this book to my children as a record of what I did in their financial literacy journey; and
- To share my ideas and thinking with other parents of young children so that we can all make the world a better place.

Every day I am reminded of why I write this book by the piece of paper I stuck on my wall:

'Train up a child in the way he should go
And when he is old he will not depart from it'
~ Proverbs 22:6

It's the same with children. All children should have a savings goal. Having short-, medium- and long-term goals means there is always a goal to work towards. Having a savings goal to work towards reminds the children why they work to earn money.

As with any goals, every savings goal must be measured because what gets measured gets done. Once we have set our child up with a savings goal, we need to measure the child's progress towards the goal and then find ways to ensure the child sees her progress. Any progress is good progress.

I have found visually displaying a child's progress works best with young children. When they see how close they are to the end (or how much further they have to go) they are reminded of the need to work to get there. The visual display doesn't have to be elaborate or fancy. A simple chart suffices – as long as it can be seen. Put the visual display in a prominent place where your children can see it every day.

> ... every savings goal must be measured because what gets measured gets done.

Play money games

Playing money games is one of the best ways of engaging young children to learn about earning money in a fun way. One game you can play with all your children is the monthly money challenge. Make a list of daily family chores around the home that the children can complete to get paid. Encourage the children to do a chore a day so that by the end of the month, they have saved up a pre-determined amount towards their goal. You can start in any month, but choosing a month with 31 days allows you to have a conversation later on about the effect of a shorter month on their pay if the game is played in a month with fewer days. Don't forget to remind your children to save some of their pay for the long term.

> Each time we play a game, my children pick up a new skill or a new concept.

Other money games are explained below.

Board games

If you were a child growing up before online games became popular, you will remember playing board games. I have fond memories of playing board games with family and friends as a child. Looking back at those experiences, I now recognise that there were implicit skills in each game that I had unconsciously absorbed - skills such as taking turns, learning different ways to count or skip count and recognising patterns on a dice. I developed these skills over time because the game was so much fun and I wanted to keep playing them over and over again. Each time I played, it sharpened my skills a bit more. Initially I had difficulties recognising the dots on a dice as representing a certain number. Over time, I developed the skill in recognising the dot patterns for its number representation.

As I play board games with my children now, I recognise these same implicit skills. Each time we play a game, my children pick up a new skill or a new concept. I particularly like playing money board games because someone else has come up with a fun and easy way of teaching the children difficult money concepts – I simply have to play it according to its rules and instructions.

Sometimes I use money board games to start money conversations with my children. When my children were six, eight and ten years old, I wanted to find a board game that would engage my children in money concepts. There aren't a lot of board games that are suited to such a wide age range. Board games suitable for a six year old are often too boring and easy for a ten year old. Board games that are suited to ten year olds are often too difficult for a six year old. One game that suited all three of my children was *Pay Day*. Sometimes I would join them in the game just for fun. Other times I would join them with the intention of teaching them money concepts and money lessons during the game. My eldest child also enjoys playing *Game of Life* with us. Both these board games taught my children lessons about money that I hadn't thought of previously. It also taught them concepts that I would have struggled to explain. For example, I was able to explain the concept of 'value' to my children through playing *Pay Day*. For both board games, we chose the older 1970s edition to play as these editions homed in on basic skills with money. Life was relatively simpler in those days, without the complications of credit cards, personal finance and a variety of loans that are now available. It's easier to teach basic skills with simpler examples. We also play *Monopoly* and I use the game to explain about wealth creation. At the time of writing, my children are still a bit too young to really appreciate investing and wealth creation at a deeper level, but I'll be using *Monopoly* to help me teach them progressively as their understanding matures.

Pretend shop

Playing pretend shop is a popular game for many young children. They set up their own play shop and pretend to be the shop keeper. You can let them run with their own imagination or you can offer suggestions on how to run a proper shop. For example, I encouraged my children to make price tags for the items they wish to sell. Instead of pretending to hand over invisible money, I suggested that they make paper money of various denominations. I had a lot of fun playing pretend shop with my children. Sometimes a teddy bear is a customer but would later on become an item for sale! When I taught Richard (then seven years old) how to make a paper coin look somewhat realistic (put a piece of paper over the coin and colour in the paper over the coin) he proceeded to announce he was rich because he can make as much money as he wanted!

> We pretended to be the difficult customers and the children had to use their negotiation skills to convince us to buy. So many lessons were taught and learned in these games.

My children have also set up their own 'art exhibition' where they had to persuade their customers (mum and dad) to buy their paintings with real money. These were a lot of fun for both the parents and children. We pretended to be the difficult customers and the children had to use their negotiation skills to convince us to buy. So many lessons were taught and learned in these games.

Encourage specific reading

Every story book has a moral. Children's story books about money are no different. The thing I like best about children's books is that a lot of smart people have written stories that are tailored for children. The authors have spent many years mastering the art of engaging children in stories and how to explain very difficult concepts using very simple words to enchant a child. The same goes for children's books about money – someone else has put time and effort into writing a story about money just for children. Very difficult money concepts are illustrated simply and beautifully through a story book.

Young children may need to have these books read to them. I find reading story books to young children to be an absolute joy. Young children do not have preconceived ideas of what a book should be about or how they should be written. They are just glad to cuddle up to mum or dad to hear our voices and be fascinated by the pictures, colours and words on the pages. Younger children are delighted with just about any book that is read to them – even ones that we think are boring or confusing. A child's mind is like a sponge – they readily absorb any messages given to them, so the more good money messages they are given, the better equipped they will be in the future. Reading books about money to children has the added bonus that we can stop the story at any time to explain an interesting concept or to ask the children questions about the story.

> Children who read a variety of books may find new ideas on how they can earn money outside the home.

As a young child I learned the various ways of earning money from reading lots of story books – selling lemonade, garage sales, the newspaper run, baby-sitting or pet-sitting service, etc. Children who read a variety of books may find new ideas on how they can earn money outside the home. I am currently encouraging my own children to try out some of these ideas.

As our children become more competent readers and their comprehension matures, it's time to introduce them to money books written for a more mature audience. The timing of when this happens depends on you and your children. Some children are drawn to non-fiction books while others prefer fiction books. I was a bookworm and enjoyed reading as a child. However, I stuck with a predominantly fiction genre for a very long time and it wasn't until I was 20 years old that I started to enjoy reading non-fiction books. These days I prefer reading non-fiction books. One suggestion is to make non-fiction money books available for your children and when they are ready hopefully they will pick up the book from the shelf and start reading. Another way to encourage older children to read money books might be to ask the children to read a book you have chosen and then ask them to write an essay about the book. The best essay (chosen by you) will win a prize.

Summary

If we're not working for money, then we're not earning money. The earlier children understand how hard it is to earn money, the more they will appreciate their things. When they realise the amount of time and the level of effort they have to put into earning their dollar, they will complain less about what they *don't* have and start appreciating what they *do* have.

When the going gets tough, it is easy to just give up. Earning money can be hard work for the children and they will also want to give up when they perceive it to be too difficult. Taking baby steps, having visible goals to work towards and our constant encouragement and support will help them get there.

Young children find joy in most activities that they do, so have fun while teaching them about money. Play money games and read money books together. We will be building fond memories of the family time together, while simultaneously improving our children's financial literacy!

Chapter 4
EARNING IN PRACTICE

Introduction

It is one thing to espouse the wisdom of teaching children the importance of earning money, but it is quite another to actually find tasks where young children may earn money.

Because older children are capable of doing more tasks and doing them better, it's easier for an older child to find money-earning activities outside the home. Encouraging young children to earn money presents challenges. Young children aren't able to perform many tasks and of the ones they can do, often young children do not perform those tasks very well. Dusting a shelf seems simple enough, but often a young child will dust only the top surface and neglect the sides and corners.

Does this mean we should delay teaching our children about earning money until they are older? Absolutely not! Young children may not have many tasks they can complete, but starting them at an early age ensures that by the time they are old enough to do more tasks and earn more money, they have already cultivated the habit of earning and of doing the work properly. That is, when they are old enough to be employed outside the home, they contribute to the workplace from the very beginning, without having to go through much of the induction process.

This chapter gives you some ideas on what tasks young children can do to start earning money. There are tasks children as young as six years old can do. If you choose to give pocket money, this chapter will guide you to what you need in order to set up your pocket money system at home. If you choose not to give pocket money, this chapter will guide you to identify other activities your children can undertake to earn their own money.

Ideas for children to earn money

Children of nearly all ages are capable of earning money. With a bit of encouragement and input from parents, children as young as six years old can start earning money. What is important is that your child has a good attitude towards earning money. If you allow your young children to earn money outside the home, it's important that appropriate adult supervision is given.

What is important is that your child has a good attitude towards earning money.

Here are some ideas for young children to earn money from outside the home:

6 to 7 years old	8 to 9 years old	10 to 11 years old
Plant seeds and sell the seedlings later	Those listed for a 5 to 7 year old	Those listed for a 8 to 9 year old
Sell lemonade (the cuteness factor is a *mega* selling point)	Making cards to sell	Pet-sitting
Garage sales	Making jewellery to sell	Watering plants when neighbours go away
Make origami to sell	Make stress balls to sell	Taking orders for the sports canteen

12 to 13 years old
Here are some suggestions for a 12 to13 year old child to earn money: • Those listed for a 10 to 11 year old child • If your child plays an instrument, busk with a friend (make sure there is appropriate adult supervision). Your child is getting practise in playing an instrument and has the added bonus of keeping the noise outside the home! • Looking after younger children. Many parents prefer to do the grocery shopping alone, without young children in tow. Offer to mind the younger children for a short time while mum and dad run errands or do the grocery shopping. • Light housework. Children at this age are very capable of doing light housework such as vacuuming the carpet, sweeping the floors, washing the dishes, hanging out the laundry, etc.

12 to 13 years old
• Help younger children with homework or reading. Many parents are busy and tired towards the end of the day. After a long day at work, parents just want to sit back and relax for a while before they get busy with dinner. Offering to help with homework or reading to younger children will give the parents this short break. • Helping parents during the busy times. In most households today, it is only mum or dad who are home on their own to juggle the busy dinner time. Keeping younger children occupied while their mum or dad prepares dinner goes a long way to keeping the stress level down at a time when both parent and children are tired and hungry. It is also helpful to offer to do light housework while mum or dad is busy bathing younger children. • Refereeing in local sporting competitions. If your children are going to be at the venue anyway, they may as well turn up early or stay back late to do some refereeing. They already know the rules, so put that into good use. They get a chance to make the call and assert their authority as referee and get paid to do so!

The aim in this age group is to give them the skills and smarts to get a part-time job later on and do that job to a high standard. This is the time to really cement their attitude towards working and their gratitude about being given a chance. If your child is more advanced in his money knowledge, it would be a good time to introduce the concept of tax by withholding a set percentage from their 'pay' each month to be used toward improving the family life (e.g. new washing machine, new carpets, etc. if your household needs it). Whether you actually use your children's money to improve family life is entirely up to you. I would be inclined to keep aside the 'tax withheld' amount and surprise them by returning the amount to them when they get their licence and want to buy a car.

Legal age to work

Here are some suggestions for children who have reached the legal age to work to earn money.

- Those listed for a 12 to 13 year old child
- Data entry
- Babysitting
- Post Office
- Retail shops
- Supermarkets
- Christmas casuals
- Café and restaurants
- Fast food chains – KFC, Pizza Hut, McDonald's, Donut King
- Teaching dance, martial arts, etc. (if your child is good at these activities)
- Tutoring younger children in primary school, especially if your child is very good at a subject
- Basically any businesses you come across will be a good place to start.

By the time your child is of legal age to work he should be encouraged to seek outside employment. If you have been giving pocket money, you should be having a conversation with him about stopping or reducing his pocket money in anticipation of him getting a part-time job or finding other ways to earn money legally outside the home. If you wish to continue giving pocket money, it should not be your child's main source of income. We don't want to raise kidults (adults who continue to live like kids) and continuing to give children pocket money when they are able to work will only perpetuate the problem of them not wanting to find work. There is no incentive to do so if mum and dad keeps financing their lifestyle.

Pocket money: What is it?

In some countries, pocket money is called an allowance. The online English Oxford Living Dictionary (https://en.oxforddictionaries.com) defines pocket money as 'A small amount of money given to a child by its parents, typically on a regular basis.' I note with interest that the definition does not go further to specify what the child is to do with the money. The definition of earning is working for money, so giving pocket money without relating it to work is not earning. Nevertheless, pocket money is discussed in this chapter as many parents and children view pocket money as a way for children to earn money.

The definition of earning is working for money ...

Today, giving pocket money is controversial. It has remained popular with many parents, but many parents have also moved away from the belief that pocket money is the best way to improve children's financial literacy. Everyone has reasons for giving or not giving.

So should you give your children pocket money? Yes. Despite objections about giving pocket money, I think pocket money has a place in children's financial literacy. Below I address the common objections that parents have about giving children pocket money.

Objection #1: Young children don't need money

Young children have many things they want, but they don't have many things that they need. Some parents are against the idea of giving young children money because quite simply young children don't *need* money. Everything a young child needs in life is provided by the parents and anything else a child wants is for the parents to decide. Young children should not be given the freedom to buy whatever they want with money that is simply given to them.

I agree.

We shouldn't use pocket money to empower young children with the freedom to shop. No one else on this planet is going to give us free money to fulfil our shopping desires, so too with pocket money. It should not be given freely. Children's needs are very simple and it *is* the parents' responsibility to provide for everything a child *needs*. If there are things a child wants, it is a parent's prerogative to decide whether to give those things.

The reason I gave my children pocket money is because I used pocket money as a means to an end rather than an end in itself. Pocket money is one of the many tools that I use to teach my children money lessons, and some tools are more effective than others in teaching certain lessons about money. The money lessons I want to teach my children with pocket money are saving and budgeting; I don't use it to teach them how to spend their money wisely.

Young children do not *need* money, but they need to *learn* how money works in a practical sense.

Objection #2: It will send out wrong signals

It's very common for parents to tie giving pocket money with completing housework, getting good grades at school, doing their homework or even just good behaviour. If not done properly, such linkage can send the wrong signals to children that they deserve payment for every good deed that they do. At the extreme, it implies that a child should do good deeds *only if* they get an external reward. This takes away an opportunity for the child to experience the intrinsic joy of helping others and reduces the child's development of empathy and natural generosity.

> ... it is best if these competencies are derived from a child's inner rewards rather than motivated by financial or other external rewards.

Similarly, paying for good grades takes away the real reason for learning. Rather than learning to satisfy an inner curiosity or to add to their knowledge, paying for good grades replaces this with an extrinsic monetary motive. Real learning comes from inside all of us – it is our desire and curiosity that drives our passion for learning. This passion is then reflected in our competencies and the grade received is nothing more than a reflection of that competency. Some children are very competent in many things and they attain these competencies through motivation and effort. Some children are motivated by extrinsic rewards such as a trophy, medal, recognition and even money. Others are motivated by their desire to exceed their personal best each time or to learn new things. Whatever the motivation, it is best if these competencies are derived from a child's inner rewards rather than motivated by financial or other external rewards. Some children are competent in only a few things and if we want to improve a child's competency in a particular area, it is better to encourage their curiosity about that subject matter rather than use money as a motivator to improve their learning. If we want our children to attain good grades, we are better off encouraging their curiosity about the world around them and ensuring their learning journey is enjoyable, fun and intrinsically rewarding, rather than using money as a motivator. There was a line by Laura Ingalls in one of the *Little House on the Prairie* episodes where she commented that it's not a good idea to get paid for good grades because even eggs are graded! I agree. Money is a poor motivator for anything.

If not thought through properly, giving pocket money can cause a lot of angst and frustration ...

Pocket money is a very effective tool to use to teach financial literacy. However, we have to put some thought into giving pocket money before we jump into the 'giving' bandwagon. It's much more complex than simply deciding how much, when and how often to give (although none of these decisions are simple). If not thought through properly, giving pocket money can cause a lot of angst and frustration for parents and children. The ability to use pocket money to send out the correct messages and incorrect messages is the reason why parents should tailor pocket money to the family's values, beliefs and attitudes about money. One family's pocket money system will be different to another family's system. I have gone through many frustrations with pocket money with my own children and had to go back to the drawing board many times to refine my method. I now have one that works very well for my family. At the end of this chapter I explain my family's pocket money system.

Objection #3: There are other ways of teaching financial literacy

Any time there is an exchange of money is an opportunity to develop a child's financial literacy. According to this view, it's not necessary to give a young child pocket money. They can learn about money in other ways that don't involve pocket money.

I agree.

With the possible negative effects of giving pocket money and the availability of other ways to teach children financial literacy, it's understandable why parents might shy away from the whole idea of pocket money in the first place. Financial literacy isn't just about giving and receiving pocket money. This is why we have to put some thought into the concept of pocket money. Giving and receiving pocket money is simply another situation involving the exchange of money and is just another opportunity to have conversations with the children about money.

What I really like about giving pocket money to young children is that this is an opportunity that I know will present itself very frequently, starting with weekly. Just like any other fundamental skill, children must cultivate and practise financial literacy often. Giving pocket money on a weekly basis creates that opportunity to practise talking about money.

Another aspect I like about giving my children pocket money is that it's a situation that I can manufacture and control:

- I can set the rules and boundaries of the situation;
- I can make it easy or difficult;
- It allows me to be creative; and
- I can modify it.

Best of all, I have instant feedback on what is working and what is not working on a weekly basis and I can tweak my methodology as I go along.

A third reason I like pocket money is that it's real money for the children. It's their money and they have to make decisions (wise or unwise) about that money. Teaching about money in the abstract is not as effective as real life experience. Explaining why mum and dad go to work every day to earn money to pay for things has a different meaning for the child who has to earn his own money to pay for his own things, and manage his own money over time.

> Teaching about money in the abstract is not as effective as real life experience.

Pocket money: How to give pocket money?

Teaching financial literacy involves using tools to communicate a message. Pocket money is one of these tools. There are many more tools that we can use and you can read more about the various tools on the Kids Money Habits website (www.kidsmoneyhabits.com).

Correctly given, pocket money can be a very effective tool in teaching lessons about earning money, saving, spending, donating, investing and even budgeting. Receiving pocket money may not be the first time your child is exposed to a money transaction, but it's likely to be the first time the transaction affects them directly.

Unlike going to the grocery store and paying for the groceries with money given by mum and dad, receiving pocket money is real because the child gets to keep the money. The child gets to decide what to do with the money later. If they have to save to buy their favourite toy, children also learn delayed gratification in the money context.

When these skills are developed over time, your child will cultivate good money habits that will help him make good money decisions in the future. I'm a firm believer in giving children pocket money but I don't agree with the conventional way of giving pocket money. If we want to realise the benefits of pocket money, we must be prepared to put some thought into it.

The conventional way is flawed

After overcoming the hurdle of deciding whether to give pocket money, many parents will then go through what I went through when I first gave my children pocket money. I call this the conventional way.

I decided on an arbitrary amount to give. We live in one of the most expensive cities in the world (Sydney) so the dollar doesn't buy much these days. The amount of pocket money I gave my children was dictated by how much I thought they would need to buy ordinary items at the shops. I then went through the weekly ritual of handing over the money to my children. Sometimes this might be accompanied by words of wisdom such as:

- Spend it wisely;
- Don't go spending all of it;
- Don't spend it all on junk; and
- Save some for a rainy day.

Parental duty done, what's next on the list?

If this sounds familiar, I'm afraid I have bad news for you. This is *not* the most effective way to give pocket money. I learned this the hard way. A fundamental problem with this approach is that I allowed society's spending habits to dictate how much pocket money I give to my children. Instead of choosing an amount that made sense to me as a parent of young children, I allowed the price of goods and services to influence the amount my children ought to receive.

> Miscommunication is the underlying cause of a lot of angst between parent and child.

Another problem with the above approach is that we have simply thrown money at the children and hope they learn to be sensible with it. But we can't explain why one child gets a certain amount and another child gets another amount. Or why both children should get the same amount. We also haven't defined exactly what is 'sensible'. What may appear sensible to the child may be irresponsible by adult standards. Similarly, what is sensible in the adult world may appear nonsensical for the child.

To achieve a common understanding, we need to have a conversation with our children about pocket money. Miscommunication is the underlying cause of a lot of angst between parent and child. We have not set boundaries for the money, we haven't explained why we're giving them the money and we haven't set our expectations about what happens to that money once it leaves our hands. Maybe it's because we are not sure *why* we're giving them pocket money. If this is the reason, then we ought to clarify the reasons for ourselves first, before we give pocket money.

The better way to give

Giving pocket money is more than handing over an arbitrary amount every week while espousing words of wisdom to the children. If you decide to give pocket money, there are a few things you need to think about.

If you decide to give pocket money, there are a few things you need to think about.

1. When to start giving

Most children start receiving pocket money from the age of six. This is not to say that money is taboo for children under the age of six. The earlier children are exposed to money concepts, the easier it is for them to learn more complex money lessons as they grow older.

Up until the age of about six, children's exposure to money should be fun. They learn about money in the abstract – what it looks like (notes and coins), where to keep it (money box) and what they can physically do with it (spin it, roll it, fold it).

From about seven years old, children begin to understand the concept of money as something valuable. It's no longer about seeing money as an object. Now, they begin to understand money as a valuable commodity. It has the power to make things happen, like buying things. So it's now time to teach them how to be responsible with money. It is also from this age that money lessons are dictated by the child's maturity and understanding about money rather than the age of the child.

2. How much to give

One good formula to follow is to give the child $1 for each year of age: a six year old will receive $6; an eight year old will receive $8; a 12 year old will receive $12. This takes away any perceived unfairness that can arise if an amount is picked arbitrarily and randomly. By the time the child is working age, you should consider stopping or reducing the amount you give to encourage them to get a part-time job or find other ways to legally earn money outside the home.

By the time the child is working age, you should consider stopping or reducing the amount you give to encourage ...

3. How often to give

Weekly pocket money works best for children up to the age of ten years old. Decrease the frequency to fortnightly or monthly for older children because from 11 years old, children are able to exercise delayed gratification. Children in this age group should be taught how to budget to make their money stretch before they receive their next 'pay'.

Pick a day of the week where the family is not busy and spend some time talking to your children about the money as you hand over their pocket money.

4. What lessons do you want to tie to the pocket money?

Every exchange of money is an opportunity to teach or reinforce a money lesson for the children. You have the power to decide what money lessons your children will learn when you hand over their pocket money. Here are some money lessons you may wish to teach and the conversations you can have with your children.

Earning	Ask your child questions to gauge their understanding of why they are getting pocket money. Ask them how else they can fill up the money box.
Saving	Encourage your child to keep their money away safely in a money box (or bank account for older children).
Spending	Help your child decide how much of their pocket money they should set aside for saving and how much for spending.
Donating	Philanthropy is an important lesson to teach children that money can be used for a greater good. Decide as a family which charity you will support. Older children can decide if they want to support their own charity. Encourage your children to set aside some money to donate to charity.
Investing	For children 11 years and older, delayed gratification is the cornerstone of teaching the child about saving and investing. Mid-teen years are the best years to start teaching children about the concept of investing, using examples of delayed gratification. Help your child understand investing in shares by speaking to them about buying a share of the shops your family frequently visits. Online share investing games tailored to teenagers are a great way to spark their interest in investing in shares. You could also show them how compounding works by using compound interest as an example and explaining the bank statement to them.

5. What rules will you have?

Now that you have empowered your child with money, decide what rules you will have. What limits will you set to their use of the money? Discuss with them what they are allowed and not allowed to spend their money on. It's their choice, but you have the right to veto. For example, they cannot spend all their money on lollies.

Writing down these rules can be useful to resolve any future disagreements. You can add to or modify the written rules as needed. If you have more than one child, these rules serve as the consistent approach to pocket money for every child in the family.

6. When to stop giving

Pocket money is not supposed to go on forever. We don't want pocket money to hinder children finding ways to earn their own money. Nor do we want to be raising kidults or funding their adult lifestyle. It's important that you decide, at the outset, when you want to stop giving your children pocket money. This should then form part of the conversation you have with the children at the start of giving them pocket money. This sets the expectation for both the parent and the child as to when they can expect to stop getting pocket money. If you are not ready to cut off their pocket money supply on that future date, you can extend this date. It's always easier to extend the time to inflict financial pain than it is to inflict the pain itself, so setting up the expectation of an end date at the outset will minimise any angst later on.

Pocket money is one of the tools we can use to teach children about money. The timing of when to stop giving pocket depends on the lessons you want to teach your children. Money lessons that are learnt over time become a habit. Once your child has developed the habit, it's time to move onto other tools to teach other lessons and develop another habit.

Whatever your timeframe to stop giving pocket money, you should be reducing the amount you give to your child once they are old enough to work. This will encourage them to get a part-time job.

7. Don't forget the conversation

It's time to have a conversation with your children about pocket money when you:

- Know what money lessons you want to teach your children;
- Are clear on the rules for giving, using and stopping pocket money; and
- Have decided to use pocket money as the tool to teach them those lessons.

Every week or fortnight, when you hand over the pocket money to your children, check that they understand the lessons you want them to learn. Have a conversation with them each time you give them pocket money. Ask them questions to get feedback that they understand what you're teaching. For younger children, it's important that they are having fun with the pocket money tool. Lots of praise and encouragement in the beginning is the key to sustaining their habits.

Any conversation, no matter how brief, is still a conversation. It can be as short as a few minutes or it can be a few hours – be guided by your child's response and interest in the topic.

Pocket money: Tying it to household chores

Despite it being a foundation for understanding money, opinion is divided as to whether pocket money should be tied to chores. Some parents give pocket money with no strings attached. Other parents give pocket money on the condition that the children complete household chores.

> ... chores need to be done ...

Some parents believe children should do chores because they are part of the family and doing chores is helping out the family. No doubt this is one way of looking at Maslow's *Hierarchy of Needs* (mentioned briefly in Chapter 3 and discussed in more detail in Chapter 7) in pursuing the need to belong to a group. This thinking takes the view that if mum or dad cooks dinner or takes out the rubbish, no one pays them to do these chores around the home. Nevertheless they must be done, otherwise no one will be fed and the home will stink and be infested with vermin. In a similar vein, children are given responsibilities around the home because these chores need to be done for the smooth functioning of family life.

There are also parents who believe that relating chores to pocket money teaches children the concept of working for money. Just as parents work to earn money, if the children want money they must earn it by doing work around the home. This group of parents take the view that no one gets paid simply by being. Mum and dad don't get paid simply by existing in the world – to get paid in a job, we must all earn the money by working.

The approach you choose depends on what money lesson you want to teach your children. Remember, pocket money is one tool you can use to teach children money lessons. If you want your children to learn about earning money, then giving pocket money for doing housework is one way of teaching them. If you want to teach your children other money lessons that do not involve the exchange of time, skill and effort for money, then don't link pocket money with completing housework.

Paying for chores: The happy medium

There is in fact a happy medium to this debate. It's one that works brilliantly for my family. We identify 'family chores', 'contribution chores' and 'individual chores'. Individual chores are those that must be completed by the child as a personal responsibility. These chores generally benefit the child only – keeping his room tidy, making his bed, etc. – and should not be paid. Contribution chores are chores the child completes as contribution towards the family. These are chores which benefit another member of the family and can technically be categorised as family chores, however these chores are not paid. The third category, family chores are chores which, if completed by the children, will relieve the parents from doing it. Family chores in my household include feeding the family pet, doing the laundry, loading and unloading the dishwasher, etc. The latter category of chores is ones that we tie to money. This is because it relieves mum and dad from doing the chores therefore it frees up mum and dad's valuable time. The time it takes a child to complete these chores ought to be exchanged with money – these are paid chores.

Whether you have an open market for paid chores (that is, anyone can do them and whoever does it gets paid) or allocate certain family chores to each child is up to you. I prefer to allocate certain family chores to each child because I have found that sometimes, open market doesn't work – none of the children want to do it and I end up having to do it. When I allocated specific family chores to individual children, these chores get done. I also have a rule which requires the child to pay whoever completes the chore for him if he doesn't do it. This can include paying mum or dad if we have to do it.

> ... one of my children offered his allocated family chore to his sister so that his sister could reach her savings goal ...

If a child is saving up for a goal and is asking for ways to earn more money, you can then find other family chores for him to do to help him reach that goal. This would be akin to a child asking to do overtime in a real job. I also had instances where one of my children offered his allocated family chore to his sister so that his sister could reach her savings goal earlier. You can read more about this in Chapter 6.

You may wish to define very clearly what is meant by 'pocket money'. In my household, pocket money is the money that is given unconditionally to the children. Money that the children earn by completing housework is not called 'pocket money'. We call it money-for-completing-chores. It's a bit of a mouthful for now, until we come up with something shorter.

Paying for chores by other means

While writing this book, I researched the question of why parents give pocket money. The underlying theme for all the reasons I came across is that the purpose of pocket money is to teach children how to manage money. When I am asked why I give pocket money, my response is always, 'it's one of the tools I use to teach my children about money'. I am then asked whether other tools can be just as effective – for example, using screen time as 'payment' for completing chores.

> If the children want to play on their electronic devices, they must earn their screen time by doing chores.

I find it interesting that many of the parents who object to paying their children money to complete housework nevertheless reward their children with other forms of 'currency'. A popular reward is screen time, or electronics time. If the children want to play on their electronic devices, they must earn their screen time by doing chores. I experimented with using screen time as a form of payment. However, rather than earning screen time, I allowed my children to buy their screen time with the money they earned from completing chores. I abandoned that experiment after a while for two reasons. Firstly, I allowed my children limited screen time as part of their relaxation activity on the weekends (playing games on their electronics) and as part of their learning about the digital world (learning to code). Secondly, when the children know that they are allowed free screen time (though limited) they were unwilling to use their money to buy more of the screen time, so the offer was never taken up.

The justification often given for using these other forms of reward is that they remove money from being the focus of the lesson. It reinforces the children's contribution to the family rather than focusing on the monetary reward of their effort. I cannot see the logic in this. If the other forms of rewards (for example screen time, stickers, etc) are used in place of money, doesn't the focus simply shift from money to the other form of reward?

Using other rewards as a motivation tool instead of money is essentially avoiding the elephant in the room. Using other forms of reward will definitely help with teaching children the underlying habits required to manage money, but if we want our children to be financially literate, we must ultimately move to the use of real money. For example, I used a sticker reward chart when my children were very young. These were fantastic in rewarding their efforts when they were young. But as they grow up, I moved away from using sticker charts to real money because my children cannot use stickers to buy what they want in the real world. If I am to keep money lessons real for them, I need to use real money.

... if we want our children to be financially literate, we must ultimately move to the use of real money.

A more compelling reason is that the parents who use other forms of rewards are not using household chores as a way to teach their children about earning money. This is fine, as long as you find other ways of teaching the children about earning money. The best way to teach children about money is to use money. There's no point using a representation of money to teach about money.

Pocket money: How it is given in my household

In my household, we clearly distinguish between 'pocket money' in the sense of giving the children money unconditionally and 'earning money' in the sense of completing family household chores for money.

I give my children pocket money for only 12 months. Yes, that's right. They are introduced to the concept of pocket money with its associated rules on their sixth birthday. They know:

- How much money they are getting ($6);
- How often they are receiving pocket money (weekly);
- What they have to do with that money (save half, spend half);
- What they can do with the money (buy anything they want, but they must have my approval first); and
- When it will end (on their seventh birthday).

Why only 12 months? The reason is because I use pocket money as a tool to teach my children the concept of saving and budgeting. Each time they receive $6, they must put $3 into their saving box and $3 into their spending box. That's it.

I don't use pocket money to teach about earning (that is taught by paying them on completion of their allocated family chores – this is an additional payment to pocket money when the child is six years old). By the time the child is seven years old he will have practised at least 52 times of saving half, spending half. By this time, they have already developed the habit of saving half, so continuing to give pocket money no longer serves its purpose. It's now time to move on to other lessons using other tools to cultivate new money habits.

Summary

Earning money involves using our time, skills and effort to do work, so cultivating children's habits in earning money can be a challenge when our children prefer to use their time, skills and effort to play on their electronic devices or participate in social media.

But earning money is such an important lesson for our children to learn because unless they understand how difficult it is to earn money, they will not appreciate the value of money and therefore the value of the things they buy with money. The gratitude they show other people who buy them things or offer to pay for their expenses all come from understanding the hard work behind earning money.

'Opportunity is missed by most people
because it is dressed in overalls and looks like work.'
~ Thomas Edison

Chapter 5
SAVING

Introduction

Saving is a fundamental part of managing money. We teach our children to save by encouraging them to set money aside for the future. As we become more intentional in teaching our children about money, we realise that saving money is so much more than the act of setting aside money.

There are also long-term consequences for our children as they learn and cultivate the habit of saving. The mindset and behaviour involved in cultivating this habit affects other areas of our children's lives now, and well into adulthood.

Encouraging the habit of saving is an important aspect of a child's financial literacy, but if not done carefully, our children's careful saving habits can turn into hoarding behaviour. There is a way of ensuring our children don't become the next Ebenezer Scrooge and it's easier than you think!

This chapter explores the concept of what saving entails and explains how teaching our children to save money may affect other areas of their life. Long-term wealth creation doesn't depend on how much is earned, but on how much is saved.

What is saving?

Today's consumer society encourages buying now rather than waiting to buy. While many if not most parents dislike the buy now mindset, it is accepted as a reason why it's difficult to teach our children about saving. We assume this readiness to consume means that children are becoming increasingly incapable of grasping the concept of saving.

It may come as a surprise that many children already have an in-built ability to save. We cultivated their foundation to be good savers a long time ago, when our children were toddlers. Let's analyse the concept of saving in a deeper sense.

> ... many children already have an in-built ability to save.

Waiting to spend

We often think about saving in terms of setting money aside and adding to the balance until we have enough for what we want. So when we teach our children to save, we encourage them to put aside small amounts frequently over time until they have enough for what they want to buy. This is essentially teaching children to defer their consumption. It is teaching them that if they defer their consumption of small items now – such as chocolates, lollies and ice creams – and keep that money they did not spend in their savings box, they will have enough money to able to buy the bigger things they want in the future. I asked my children to explain to me what 'saving' meant and their reply was the same – putting money aside until they have enough to buy what they want.

Deferred consumption involves a delay between having money and spending that money. From a very young age, we teach our children to wait for their turn. Wait for their turn on the swing, wait to speak, wait in line at the grocery store, etc. Waiting is a key attribute of saving and children experience this on a daily basis. Every time we ask our children to wait we are cultivating their habit to save. Teaching children the concept of saving is therefore not new and it is not a difficult concept to learn.

> The difference between idle time and saving lies in what we do while we wait.

While saving involves waiting, it is not just waiting. If we simply waited, the only thing that happens is time passes us by. If a child wanted to buy a brand new Lego set, simply waiting for it won't result in her getting that Lego set. Something must happen in that waiting time. The difference between idle time and saving lies in what we do while we wait. We must use that time to continue to earn money. Saving is the habit involving two elements:

- Spending less than we earn and therefore being able to set aside some of the money that we earn; and
- Waiting until we have accumulated enough money to spend on what we were saving up for.

Reduced spending

Another aspect of saving is reducing the amount we spend. Just because we have put aside enough of the amount we need is no reason to go spending all of that money straight away. Teaching our children to search for a better deal is part of cultivating their saving habit. It is also part of cultivating wise spending, which is discussed in Chapters 7 and 8. If an item can be bought at a lower price the difference between the amount that was set aside for the item and what was eventually spent to buy the item is also a saving. At the extreme end, if the amount spent on the item is reduced to zero (i.e. we no longer want the item or we can get the item for free) then whatever is not spent now is also a saving.

> Teaching our children to search for a better deal is part of cultivating their saving habit.

Reduce spending on groceries

Learning to make things at home is one way of reducing the amount we spend, except for ingredients and materials needed to make the item. The family's grocery list is the most obvious and most effective way to teach children about reducing the household spending and therefore saving money.

Before I learned how to make yoghurt at home, I often bought tubs of yoghurt (always when it's discounted). When I became aware of the sugar content of store-bought yoghurt, I decided I didn't want my children eating these any more. I learned to make my own yoghurt at home and was amazed at how easy it was. So I started a conversation with my children about learning to make items that we consume regularly, starting with food. The more food we learn to make ourselves, the more items we can cross off our shopping list, thus saving money. But life is never quite as simple as this. Sometimes, we might be able to save more by buying the food instead of making it at home. For example, if it takes one hour to prepare food at home, someone who earns a high income may be financially better off to work that hour instead of preparing food. The amount she earns will cover the cost of the food (and any other costs associated with working that hour) and if there is money left over afterwards to put towards her savings, it will be more economical for her to work rather than prepare her own food at home in that hour. To complicate things further, some high income earners may nevertheless choose to use that one hour to prepare food at home because she enjoys cooking and finds it relaxing, whereas working more may lead to more stress. All of these would make good money conversations too!

Teaching children to make things also involves teaching them that sometimes we have to spend in order to save. Initially I wasn't keen on making my own yoghurt because the few times I tried were unsuccessful. I subsequently found out the reason was simply because I didn't have the necessary tools to make yoghurt successfully and easily. Then I bought a yoghurt maker for $20 and followed the instructions. Once I was successfully making yoghurt, there was no turning back.

Home-made things may not always lead to a saving. In the yoghurt example, I had to explain to the children that while making yoghurt at home reduced the amount I spent on yoghurt tubs every month, I still had to buy the ingredients to make yoghurt – the milk powder and yoghurt culture. In this example, the cost of these ingredients was far less than the cost of buying tubs of yoghurt each time. In other examples, it may not work out to be cheaper – such as buying a cow in order to produce our own milk.

Reduce spending on hidden costs

Many of our daily activities involve spending on things we don't notice. We are so reliant on using commodities such as electricity, gas and water that we automatically pay these bills without much thought. Many people resign themselves to the fact that there is not much they can do about these costs because maintaining our standard of living is a necessary cost.

I have found talking about these hidden costs to be one of the best ways of teaching my children about saving money through reducing the amount we spend. The first time I showed my children our quarterly electricity and gas bills I explained that these are charged on a user-pays basis. The more we use gas and electricity, the more we have to pay. I also showed them that electricity costs more than gas, so substituting gas for electricity reduces the amount we spend on heating and lighting.

Using the bills was also another way for me to explain why I have certain rules in the home, such as switching off the TV at the wall, unplugging appliances when not in use and switching off the freezer when we go on a holiday. I have also removed light bulbs from their sockets in areas of the home where we don't really need bright light. Without these bills to help explain the reasons for my rules, my children may think I'm just a weird mum who insists on quirky rules.

When my children understood that gas is cheaper than electricity, I took this opportunity to explain this is why we no longer have a kettle to boil water. We use a saucepan instead. Our electric kettle decided to call it a day after ten years of service and we decided not to buy a replacement. Lack of space was another reason for not replacing the item. I was also able to explain to them the daily cost of using electricity and gas and how many aspects of our daily activities have hidden costs. The long showers they have every day uses electricity. The first time David heard this at six years old, he was surprised as he thought electricity was only for lights. I explained to him the hot water he's using has to be heated up and in the absence of solar power, we rely on electricity to heat up the water.

Electricity is used unnecessarily when:

- the curtains are closed during the day and lights must be used;
- someone forgets to switch off the lights when leaving the room; and
- someone forgets to switch off the toaster or the television at the power point after use.

My thinking is that if the oven has to be on, then it may as well have both shelves full and cooking at the same time.

Elisabeth loves to bake, but she only bakes one muffin tray each time. We have a big oven with two shelves and I usually like my oven working at full capacity each time it is used. My thinking is that if the oven has to be on, then it may as well have both shelves full and cooking at the same time. Whenever my daughter bakes muffins, I always throw in a tray of pies or sausage rolls, lasagne, pasta bake, apple crumble – anything, just to fill up the remaining space in the oven. Elisabeth now understands the reason I do this is because I like to get the most out of oven time.

Why we should teach children about saving

Delayed gratification

The underlying habit in long-term wealth creation is delayed gratification. If we are willing to forgo many of our wants or luxuries today, we will be able to enjoy more of what we want and more of life's luxuries later. Sometimes the more we are willing to delay our gratification today the quicker that 'later' time comes.

One aspect of saving is teaching children patience. This is something we have already taught our children when they were toddlers. Without knowing it, we have set our children up with a very good foundation for saving.

Unfortunately, as children grow older, the consumer society doesn't present much opportunity to practise delayed gratification. The internet and mobile technology means information and communication is readily available, shortening the time we need to wait for almost anything.

> ... the consumer society doesn't present much opportunity to practise delayed gratification.

Having a mobile phone allows us to call each other instantaneously. Children are given mobile devices to entertain them while they wait in queues, wait for public transport or wait for their meals in restaurants. My children are given iPads at the hairdressers to watch cartoons while getting their hair cut. I have since learned how to cut hair, so I now cut my children's hair at home. Rather than have them watch cartoons on the iPad or TV, I have money conversations with them instead, while cutting their hair!

Many people want things now and are not willing to go without in order to have what they want in the future. We have become so accustomed to this instant result that we now expect it in other areas of society. We are witnessing increasing levels of impatience everywhere, and this will not serve our children well when we come to teach them about responsible spending. They will not have cultivated patience to wait and research their desired products before purchasing.

There is a saying that I teach my children:

'If you will live like no one else, later you can live like no one else.'
~ Dave Ramsey

What Dave Ramsey means in a more practical sense is to be willing to save now when others indulge so that we can indulge later when no one else can. This is really difficult for children, especially in their teenage years when peer acceptance is so important.

> ... to be willing to save now when others indulge so that we can indulge later when no one else can.

This is why my book is written for parents of children between ages six and twelve years old. I firmly advocate for children in this age group to be taught good money habits, before peer influence really kicks in. Children who have been taught good money habits have a solid foundation to stand on when they face the turbulent teenage years later.

True wealth creation comes from delayed gratification. If children do not practise delayed gratification when they are young, it becomes more difficult to form this habit when they are older and peer pressure becomes more intense. Adults who do not practise delayed gratification don't become wealthy later. Earning a high income does not create wealth if we simply spend it all as soon as we have the money.

> Adults who do not practise delayed gratification don't become wealthy later.

Appreciation

Children who saved to pay for their toys or outings are more appreciative of their toys or outing experience. It was the same with my children. Previously, when we took them out for a family outing, my children would often find something to complain about. However, when I started to ask them to save up for an outing, they became more appreciative of the experience. I noticed they complained less about queues, the crowd, how hot or cold it was etc. A reminder about how hard everyone else in the family has saved for the trip is usually enough to stop them feeling sorry for themselves and start appreciating other people's efforts.

It's the same with toys. When my children saved to buy their own toys, they were more careful with their toys. Instead of carelessly tossing the toys aside when they are finished playing, they carefully packed them away. Instead of being rough when playing with those toys, they generally looked after the toys better. If they misplaced or lose a toy, they no longer have the attitude of 'we'll just buy another one' because they know how long they had to save to buy that toy.

Antidote to a sense of entitlement

The now culture is slowly but surely creating a sense of entitlement in our society. It is why we witness so many more tantrums in children these days. It is not only children who are slowly being poisoned by this. Adults are equally affected. I believe it is also why we are witnessing many more incidents of adults behaving impatiently or aggressively. There are a lot more narky comments made towards each other, anger when someone cuts in front of us, cheap sniping remarks when someone else is chosen for a promotion over us and a general impatience to wait for things. Common courtesy and consideration for others was the norm, but such behaviour is increasingly replaced by selfishness and a sense of entitlement.

> Delayed gratification is a habit that has to be practised and cultivated over time. All our teaching about patience and waiting will not come to fruition if children are not given the opportunity to practise patience and waiting.

Delayed gratification changes the way we think about having to wait for things. Instead of feeling as if we are being robbed of our time, we instead appreciate the intense satisfaction we will have when we reach our goal. We know there is a reason for the delay (we're working hard and saving), we know we have to wait and we know it will be worth it because there is gratification at the end of the long delay.

Delayed gratification is a habit that has to be practised and cultivated over time. All our teaching about patience and waiting will not come to fruition if children are not given the opportunity to practise patience and waiting. The more we practise delayed gratification, the more we anticipate the reward that comes from all that waiting. Without practise, the wait is simply a delay without gratification. As with all habits that we want our children to develop, we must also self-reflect on our own behaviour when there is delay. Do we get angry and show our frustrations to the children or do we take this as an opportunity to practise patience and waiting?

> A promotion is the delayed gratification.

Removing our children's sense of self-entitlement will have a much bigger reward later in life when our children enter the workforce. Many young people fall into the trap of wanting to climb the corporate ladder quickly. If they don't get there quickly, they start looking for reasons why they haven't got there. They take the high moral ground with comments like 'I didn't get the promotion because I don't play politics'. Other comments are more toxic to the heart – the boss plays favouritism; the person who got promoted is such a brown nose; it's a male/female/race thing; it's because I am the primary carer of the family and so I can't be there to pander to the boss's requirements. Again, no doubt there may be truth in some or all of these, but more often than not, the unsuccessful candidate doesn't reflect on the fact that perhaps she simply doesn't have enough experience for that role and experience comes with time and exposure. A promotion is the delayed gratification.

Effect on other children

When I became more intentional in teaching my children about money and developing good money habits, my only goal was (and is) that they will be sensible with their money. My vision is that my children be financially independent at a young age. Why? Because during my thirties, I reached a point where I questioned my purpose in life. I came across a quote: 'Are you an observer in life or are you a participant?' and realised that I had been an observer for a very long time, and decided that I wanted to be a participant. But what was I meant to do with my life? What is my purpose, my legacy, my calling? I realised then that whatever they are, I am now in a position to start participating in life. One reason I could do so was because I was brought up with good money habits and this has enabled me to choose the next stage in my life. I am not yet at a stage where I can give up work completely, but I don't need to worry too much about where my next pay is going to come from, at least in the short- to medium- term. In the quest to clarify my next move, I spoke to many people in their mid- to late-30s and early-40s and was surprised to learn that many people have felt or are feeling the way I felt. This stage in life is also called a mid-life crises or an awakening. Given the number of people I know who have gone through or going through this stage in life, I anticipate my children may also come to this point in their lives eventually. If so, I would like my children to be in the same or a better position as I am to pursue their interests without worrying too much about finance.

One thing was for certain – it was never my intention for my lessons to reach beyond my children.

One day, Richard (then nine years old) told me one of his classmates asked him why he uses old bread bags to wrap up his sandwiches. Another classmate overheard the question and replied that the reason we do it is because we want to save money. When Richard relayed this story to me, I wasn't sure how I felt about this because I wasn't sure how Richard would feel about the answer. When I was his age, I would have been embarrassed by the reply. I would feel that the child who replied saw me as poor – so poor that we can't even afford to buy proper cling wrap for the sandwich. So I asked Richard cautiously how he felt about the reply and

Richard said that he was fine with it. He said it's true that we save money by not buying cling wrap and reused other plastic bags instead. He is a very matter-of-fact person and I wasn't convinced that he was okay with his classmate's response, so I played devil's advocate and suggested that we should start buying cling wrap for school lunches. He stared at me in disbelief then said, 'Why would you want to do that? Buying plastic just to wrap up food and then throw it away, when we already have plastic we can use?! That's like throwing away money!'

... it would appear the old adage of 'more is caught than taught' has in fact been caught on by other children!

So despite me not intending to extend my children's money lessons farther, it would appear the old adage of 'more is caught than taught' has in fact been caught on by other children! I'm sure the child lunching with Richard would have had a discussion with his parents about Richard's lunches being wrapped in bread bags.

Environmentally friendly saving

I advised Richard that my real reason for reusing bread bags is more for environmental reasons rather than financial reasons, but I used saving money as the reason when explaining to my children why we use existing plastics bags instead of cling wraps.

I'm an environmentalist. I hate to throw things out and teach my children to keep things that can be reused or recycled. Over time, I realised that being conscious of how our actions affect the environment are consistent with saving money. The lessons we teach our children about savings inevitably lead us to take actions that reduces our consumption of things that are harmful to the planet.

Using the lesson about deferring consumption as an example, sometimes waiting to save up for what we thought we really wanted can have the effect of tempering our desire. By the time we have saved up enough, we find that we no longer want the item. The less stuff we buy, the less stuff ends up in landfill and the less pollution is emitted by making the stuff. Saving and waiting to buy the item also has the effect that we appreciate the item a lot more and we are not so willing to throw it away.

> The less stuff we buy, the less stuff ends up in landfill and the less pollution is emitted by making the stuff.

Another example where my family have reduced our environmental impact is making our own yoghurt pouches. For a very long time, despite knowing how to make yoghurt, I was still buying yoghurt pouches for my children's lunch boxes. Not only were the pouches adding unnecessary expenses to my grocery bill, I was also concerned about the environmental impact when the pouches were used once and then thrown into the bin; they are not recyclable. I started to look for ways to reuse the yoghurt pouches and finally came across an online company that sold reusable pouches. Now my home-made yoghurt is put into reusable pouches for the children to take to school. I had to buy those re-fillable pouches, but I saved money in the long term by not having to buy any more yoghurt pouches. The amount we saved in eliminating yoghurt pouches from our grocery list has more than paid for the cost of the pouches. Reusing the pouches has also reduced our negative impact on the environment.

Walking is something I love to do now. I find that the more I walk, the easier it becomes and the more I enjoy walking. I am often surprised at how much faster walking can be compared to taking public transport, especially when I know the short cuts. Not only do I avoid traffic and the hassles with finding parking, I am also saving on petrol costs as well as the environment. Despite living very close to our local school, my children often ask to be driven to school. Sometimes it's because they simply don't want to walk, sometimes they are tired ('my little legs can't walk far today') and sometimes it's because they want more time at home to play with their toys before going to school. Just as often, my reply is that we're walking, for the reasons I mentioned earlier – it's better for the environment, better for our health and it saves on petrol and other running costs. More often than not, I also prove that walking to school is actually faster than driving because we cut through buildings when we walk whereas we'd drive around the same buildings if we went by car.

Lessons in being more environmentally friendly with our actions can result in lessons about savings.

In a casual conversation with my children one day, I mentioned that sustainable living can be compatible with saving money. David (then six years old) asked what sustainable meant. I explained that it means the living thing continues to exist and will never become extinct. Later that evening, while I was preparing dinner, David came into the kitchen and said, 'Mummy, I wish you were sustainable'. Elisabeth (then 11 years old) overheard the comment and remarked, 'Yeah, I think we all do, mummy'.

I may not have been successful in explaining the meaning of 'sustainable' that day, but I sure felt lots of love!

Saving vs hoarding

'It is the love *of money that is the root of all kinds of evil.'*
~ Timothy 6:10

Saving and hoarding involve keeping money in a safe place for the longer term. Saving is good and hoarding is bad. What is the difference between saving and hoarding? The difference is in the mind and the intentions of the person and what that person eventually does with the money. Our attitudes, beliefs and views about money dictate whether we have a love of money. What is our reason for making more money and keeping as much as possible? We never want our children to grow up to be like Ebenezer Scrooge before he was visited by the ghosts of Christmas past, present and future. Scrooge was someone who had a love of money. He was a money hoarder.

> Our attitudes, beliefs and views about money dictate whether we have a love of money.

How do we make sure our children are savers and not hoarders? One way is to ensure the children know why they are saving their money. Having a goal or a purpose with money changes the action from hoarding to saving. Saving is working towards achieving a goal. The goal might be to buy something, to have a more balanced life, or to donate it to charity. It could be saving for a better future, to achieve financial independence and be able to retire from full-time employment as soon as possible. It could be simply to have a cash reserve to buy something that is unknown now, to feel comfortable knowing that such items can be bought when we need it. Saving is basically working towards a goal, whatever that goal may be. On the other hand, hoarding, is accumulating money for the sake of accumulating it, without any reason or purpose other than an unwillingness to part with money. The mindset of a hoarder is that of 'not enough' – there is not enough money. In fact, for a hoarder, there is *never* enough money. Hoarding is the love of money, which is a very dangerous habit to form because it is where all kinds of evil grow.

Teaching the difference between saving and hoarding is especially important if you have a child who is a natural saver. For a natural saver, parting with money doesn't come easily. Natural savers are happy to go without even the smallest unnecessary spending so it is not easy to convince a natural saver to spend.

> ... the difference between saving and hoarding is especially important if you have a child who is a natural saver.

My son Richard is a natural saver. He works hard at his chores and he is very careful to save most of what he earns. Beyond his basic needs, he doesn't want for much. He doesn't covet the latest brands or toys and he doesn't notice his peers' latest gadgets. He doesn't succumb readily to peer pressure. He is a very practical person and doesn't fall for cute-looking or cool-looking items. This can sometimes be difficult for a parent to deal with emotionally. I would like to see my children enjoy a treat every once in a while, but when my natural saver refuses the treat and reasons that it's just a waste of money to buy sweet stuff that will just rot his teeth, I am torn between being proud of his understanding and reasoning and saddened by his unwillingness to treat himself. I am torn between reinforcing the message that this is a good saving habit and convincing him that sometimes it is okay to spend.

The only time Richard wanted something really badly was when he was four years old. He really wanted a stuffed yellow Angry Bird – this was before the Angry Birds movie was made. He saved up all his money over a few months for $12. This was a lot of money for a four year old who earns money from doing household chores. When he finally had enough, he brought his money box with $12 in coins to ToysRUs and bought the stuffed toy. Five years later and 'Big Yellow' is still very much loved by my little boy. Big Yellow accompanies him every time we go on holiday and every time we go camping. Because he doesn't want many things, he doesn't spend his money readily. Those who have watched the Angry Bird movie will know Big Yellow's real name is Chuck.

A natural saver doesn't enjoy buying many material things. He doesn't experience the same joys from shopping the way a natural spender would find shopping therapeutic. A natural saver will only spend when he sees a good reason to part with his money.

> ... I don't want to convey the wrong message to my children that if we can justify all of our expenditures, then that spending is wise.

To ensure my natural saver doesn't turn into a hoarder, I had to teach Richard about good reasons for spending money. This wasn't easy for me because I see so many natural spenders today and I don't want to convey the wrong message to my children that if we can justify all of our expenditures, then that spending is wise. Keeping up with the Joneses is a justification, but is still unwise spending. In explaining good reasons for spending money, I had to make sure this discussion was just between me and Richard because I didn't want my natural spender children to receive a distorted message.

Richard already intrinsically knows that spending money on more stuff is not a wise decision. I explained to Richard the difference between a saver and a hoarder. This allowed me to reinforce the importance of having savings goals all the time, because without such goals, we are simply hoarding. I also explained that the goals can be saving money to spend on pursuing his interests and hobbies (he's really interested in computer coding, robotics and Lego) or to explore new interests and hobbies.

Philanthropy is another way to ensure our natural saver does not become a hoarder. Philanthropy is a good reason for saving money and a good reason for a natural spender to part with his money. Make sure you involve your natural saver in selecting the charity to donate to. It is important that we explain to our young children how the chosen charity will use their money. If we can find ways to allow the child to experience first-hand the works of that charity, it will be a more powerful message.

I support a number of charities and non-profit organisations. One charity that I have supported for a very long time is the Humour Foundation (the Clown Doctors). When I began to have a conversation with my children about charity, I explained to them my reasons for choosing the charity. I also took them to meet the Clown Doctors so that they can see first-hand the works that these Clown Doctors do. I read to my children letters that were written by sick children in the hospital, children who were the same age as my children. This allowed my children to have a more holistic understanding of what the Humour Foundation does. Over time, I have encouraged my children to put aside some of what they earn to donate to the Humour Foundation.

Summary

Saving money involves much more than waiting to spend money. But waiting for the reward at the end of a long delay is a big component to cultivating a saving habit. To ensure our children do not see the delay as an inconvenience, we must purposefully engage them in conversations about the gratification at the end of the delay. It is the sense of achievement and pride at the end that replaces an entitlement attitude in children with a sense of appreciation.

Saving money is the action of putting aside some money for the future. But the same action of putting aside money for the future can also be classified as hoarding, with the only difference being the mindset of the saver. If we cultivate our children's mindset in saving money, we cultivate a habit of saving rather than hoarding.

Chapter 6
SAVING IN PRACTICE

Introduction

Goals keep us accountable and motivated. Helping our children set savings goals and encouraging them towards achieving their goals not only keeps them motivated in saving, it also teaches children the process and purpose of goal setting in life.

This chapter explains the purpose of having savings goals, the different types of goals and how to track progress. The tools you will need to keep the children's money safe while they save are also discussed. Finally, this chapter suggests ways to keep the whole process fun and visible as further encouragement for our children to save.

Savings goals

Having savings goals gives the child a purpose on what he is working towards. Depending on the duration of the goals, they also teach children different lessons. As with any goals, it's good to have short-, medium- and long-term saving goals.

Short-, medium- and long-term goals

To cultivate our children's saving habits, we start with their short-term goals. This is where children learn what goal setting is about and that saving money has a reward at the end – the coveted item. Short-term goals teach children there is gratification at the end of the delay.

Once our children understand goal setting – the process, purpose and the rewards at the end – we move on to encourage them to achieve medium-term goals. Medium-term goals teach children that more expensive items take longer to own. With time and perseverance, those goals will eventually be achieved. Waiting stretches the children's patience a little, but also validates their belief in the goal-setting system that there *is* still gratification at the end of the delay. They just need to work towards it and persevere.

Waiting stretches the children's patience a little, but also validates their belief in the goal-setting system ...

When we are certain the children understand medium-term goals it's time to introduce long-term goals. Depending on the age and financial maturity of our children, it may be a while, even a few years, before we can successfully introduce our children to the concept of long-term goals. We may find that we have to re-introduce the concept a few times while we test our children's maturity and understanding. If the timing is not yet right, we can either encourage our child to persevere or we can decide it's simply too early and revert to the shorter term goal. Wait to reintroduce the longer term goal at a later time. It's okay if our child doesn't understand the long-term goal concept by age 12. Just introduce it later.

> Long-term goals teach children that the end result cannot be the only motivator.

Long-term goals teach children that the end result cannot be the only motivator. The nature of long-term goals is that they take a very long time to achieve. Many young children cannot fathom long-term goals because that future time is too far away. It is a time that will eventually come but it's too abstract to be meaningful for young children. While medium-term goals affirms perseverance to reach a goal, perseverance alone will not sustain the motivation and effort to reach a long-term goal. Without more, perseverance alone can lead to burn-out. This is the opportunity to teach our children to find intrinsic motivators to keep them on track to achieving their long-term goal. Teaching our children to pause and reflect on their progress in developing other life skills, insights they have gained about themselves along the way or even why the end result is their goal may be other forms of motivators that will encourage them to continue working towards their long-term goals.

'The journey is the reward.'
~ Steve Jobs, co-founder of Apple Inc.

What constitutes short-, medium- and long-term goals depend on the child's age and maturity. A short-term goal for a ten year old child is likely to be a long-term goal for a five year old. The general rule is that a short-term goal is one that is easily achieved and doesn't take much time or effort to be rewarded. For very young children, this could be one day. For older children, this could be one week to one month. The key to a short-term goal is that the child is guaranteed to achieve the goals without much time or effort.

In contrast, a long-term goal is one that will stretch the child to his limits. The goal has a time that a child thinks is almost impossible. For very young children, a long-term goal may be one month and for older children, it could be one or even five years. The idea is that a long-term goal is something a child thinks is impossible to achieve given their level of patience.

A medium-term goal is a goal that fits somewhere between a short-term goal and a long-term goal. A medium-term goal is not easily achieved but also not so difficult that it seems beyond reach for the child. A child knows that the medium-term goal can be achieved with a bit of time, effort and perseverance.

> For very young children, a long-term goal may be one month and for older children, it could be one or even five years.

Achieving short-, medium- and long-term goals

The first few times children try to save towards a short-term goal should be a success. We want to reinforce to the children that goals are achievable. We want to encourage our children to work towards their goal to realise the rewards. This may involve giving your child a bonus payment to help him achieve that goal. Be clear what the bonus payment is for – it could be a reward for doing the job efficiently; or it could be a reward for doing the job with great attitude. Whatever your reason, be sure to communicate it to your child and make it clear that it is a one-off payment that is not to be expected every time. Also make sure that it's not an I-feel-sorry-for-you payment or I'm-helping-you-get-there payment. Even though it is in fact a bonus to help him achieve the goal, we want to convey it in such a way to ensure it is a payment for other reasons, not just to get him across the line.

> Once he achieves his short-term goals a few times, we need to take a step back.

It is very tempting for parents to come to their children's rescue if it looks as if they are unlikely to achieve their goal. However, it is important that our children are allowed to learn the consequences of not reaching their goal within the expected timeframe. If we have ensured his success at reaching his short-term goals and we are getting feedback that he understands the concept of saving for a goal, it is now time to let him work it out for himself. Once he achieves his short-term goals a few times, we need to take a step back. This might mean no longer giving him that little bit of bonus. If he doesn't achieve his short-term goal within the expected timeframe, it simply means he either has to miss out or wait a bit longer to get the reward while everyone else enjoys the benefits now. This will become a lesson about Dave Ramsey's 'living like no one else will live' or it will be a lesson about delaying his gratification a bit longer in order to achieve the short-term goal.

It is the same process with achieving medium-term goals. We want to ensure their success the first few times they work towards their medium-term goals. The idea is that we want them to understand that while medium-term goals cannot be achieved as easily as short-term goals, they are achievable if the child perseveres. Once they understand this concept, we again must take a step back. Allow them to set their own medium-term goals and then allow them to get there themselves – or not. This time, we won't be helping them with bonuses, but we can cheer them on from the sidelines.

> Allow them to set their own medium-term goals and then allow them to get there themselves – or not.

Long-term goals may be very daunting – it seems impossible to achieve because it's so far away or it's too big an amount. For these goals, decide whether you will match your children's saving. For example, some parents will match their children's saving towards an expensive toy. If a child has saved up $50 towards a toy, the parents will match $50 so the child has $100 to buy the toy. Matching the saving can have the added effect of letting your child know that they are not alone in this journey. You're there with them along the way and you're in it for the long haul, which is, after all, a long-term goal.

After a family camping trip, Elisabeth declared her love for horses and she'd be in heaven if she could ride horses every day. When we returned home, I found a horse riding camp where she can in fact ride and look after her own horse for a week. It would cost $1100. Elisabeth was very interested and tried many ways to convince us to pay for the camp – can it be her birthday present?

How about birthday and Christmas present combined? How about her 'graduation from primary school' present? Nope, nope and nope.

I made her a deal – if she can save up $500 towards the camp, I'll match the other $600. I also explained that the camp is seven months away and that if she isn't able to save up that much or if the camp is booked out by the time she has enough, then she'll just wait another year to do the camp. At the time of writing this book, she is still saving up towards this goal. Whether she continues to save up towards this long-term goal will depend on her internal motivation to save, rather than the end reward of horse riding itself.

Having goals forces a child to think about whether he wants to achieve his goal sooner or whether he wants to indulge now. It is a trade-off between instant and delayed gratification.

Whether she continues to save up towards this long-term goal will depend on her internal motivation to save ...

Track progress

Children get told so many different things and rules from so many people that sometimes we're not sure if they are actually listening to us. Their minds are so busy working out how the world works and enjoying the novelty of life that even if they were listening to us, they will sometimes forget what we said. They need constant reminders. It is difficult for parents to know whether we have exhausted our oral communication. There's a fine line between a nag and a reminder. If we repeat something too often, it eventually becomes noise to our children. But if we don't remind them often enough, they forget. Inevitably, we end up frustrated with our children – either because they don't seem to listen any more or they forget what we have just said to them. So it's a good idea to have other forms of communication with our children when it comes to money matters.

> Having a visual aid to track a child's saving progress works very well.

One very effective method of communicating lessons about saving is visual aids. Children are visual people. Having a visual aid to track a child's saving progress works very well. It serves as a reminder to the children of what it is they are saving towards and shows them how close (or how far) they are from their goal. A visual aid means we don't have to orally remind them all the time – the reminder is there for the child to see. Of course it helps if the visual aid is placed in a prominent place where the child sees it every day. One suggestion is to put it on the wall in front of where the children eat their meals. That way, they are reminded of their progress at least two or three times a day. Make sure the visual aid is updated as the children make progress in their goals.

Individual goals vs family goals

I spent a lot of time thinking about whether I should implement individual saving goals and family saving goals as separate goals. Having individual saving goals means each child has ownership and responsibility in reaching his own goals. There is more accountability in achieving the goals and hence its own individual consequences when the child doesn't reach that goal, or better still, rewards when the child reaches the goal.

The downside is that sometimes these goals may work to discourage co-operation amongst the children and, worse still, sabotage. There is no common goal that everyone is working towards and this can create a hostile competition of each-for-their-own mentality.

Alternatively, family goals remove all the negative aspects associated with having individual saving goals. Family goals encourage co-operation, encouragement and a sense of togetherness. On the downside, there is no accountability and one child may end up contributing more towards the saving than another. Younger children may not notice this, but older children will recognise the unfairness or even take advantage of the younger children's willingness to contribute more.

> Family goals encourage co-operation, encouragement ...

I resolved this by combining both. For now, the goal-setting method I adopt works for my children. Whether it works for older children in their teenage years remains to be discovered. I pick family holidays as the saving goals for my family. The cost of the holiday is split into fixed costs and variable costs. The parents are responsible for all fixed costs and the children are responsible for the variable costs. Fixed costs are costs of basic necessities such as the cost of accommodation, transport, main meals, etc. Variable costs are costs that are optional. Variable costs include the costs of activities, desserts, snacks, etc. The idea is that the children save for their own variable costs. How much each child needs to save up depends on what the child wants to do. The more activities the child wants to do or the more desserts the child wants to eat, the more he will have to save up towards those costs.

My family go camping once a year. At the camp site there are activities that cost extra, like horse riding. The cost of the campsite is a fixed cost, as is the food that we bring to the camp site. However, the cost to ride a horse is variable and depends on how many times the children want to go for a ride. In drawing up our savings goal, I separated the fixed costs (paid by the parents) from the variable costs (paid by the children). This has worked very well because there are activities that my boys love doing but my daughter doesn't and vice versa. Being a variable cost also means that if a child hasn't saved up enough he will have to forgo that part of the activity. So far, there have not been complaints of any unfairness in the process or amounts.

I have also found that having individual goals set within family goals has encouraged my children to help each other reach their goals. One of the rules we have as a family is that the children must save half of all money they receive. That half is to be put away until they are an adult. The other half is for them to budget as they please, including saving up towards their goals. As explained in Chapter 4, my children are given pocket money for only twelve months, starting on their sixth birthday. Being the youngest, at age six, my son David was the only one still receiving pocket money. Out of $6 he received as pocket money, he had $3 every week to put towards his savings goals. There isn't much that a six year old can do – if we went to an amusement park, there are limited rides for him to go on due to his height and age. The cost of his entry tickets to many venues is also cheaper due to his age. Add to this the fact that he has a constant stream of 'income' by way of pocket money, he is often the first of our three children to achieve his individual saving goals. The older children, on the other hand, often have a higher amount to save towards. This is because their costs are usually higher due to their age - entry tickets are more expensive and they have a wider range of activities that they can do. As their only income is the chores they complete or items they sell, it often takes my older children longer to achieve their individual savings goal.

... I had a conversation with him about the difference between a hand-up and a hand-out.

One time, David had saved up for his goal for a family holiday but his sister was lamenting on how much more she had to save up to reach her goal. (She conveniently left out the reason being she had spent most of her money on an iPod earlier that year.) David initially wanted to help pay for his sister's share of the family holiday, but I had a conversation with him about the difference between a hand-up and a hand-out. We both agreed a hand-up was a better way to help. So I asked David how he can give his sister a hand-up. His face lit up when he replied 'I know! She can do my chores and get paid for them instead of me!' I thought it was a brilliant idea – so did his sister.

Having individual goals also empowers children to decide which activities they will do and how often, within their own budgets. It helps them prioritise how they use their money. It took my son Richard a few months to save up for two hours of horse riding for the camping trip. He had handed the money over to me for safe keeping until the camping trip itself. In the meantime, another activity came up, and he was expected to pay for this. He had one month to earn enough money for the other activity. Knowing how badly he wanted to do this other activity, I was tempted to help him along the way. I resisted. At the end of the month, he counted his earnings and there wasn't enough for both. Again, I was tempted to come to his rescue. Again I resisted. He sat thinking for a few minutes then told me he no longer wanted to do any horse riding at the campsite. He asked if he can have his horse riding money back to pay for the other activity. I had a conversation with him about priorities – was he sure he wanted to forgo horse riding at the campsite for this other activity. Yes. The lawyer in me couldn't resist interrogating further. Why did he want to forgo horse riding? Because there are other fun stuff to do while camping – like playing with sticks and skipping stones (and playing with sticks in the campfire) – he's not mad-keen on horses and he can always go horse riding again another time. I handed back his money and he was very happy. Not only was he be able to pay for the activity he really wanted to do, he also had some money left over for another savings goal.

Keep it safe

Teaching children how to save money will inevitably involve teaching them where to keep their money until the day they spend that money.

> ... teaching them where to keep their money ...

Use a money box

I believe the most important gift for a child to begin his journey into learning about money is the money box. It is so much more than a place to keep his money for a rainy day or for him to save up for that big toy he covets. I see the money box as a gift of financial freedom which begins with good money habits:

- The money box begins as a present – children (and adults!) love presents.
- It becomes a special place where children put their treasured money.
- It is then used as a tool to teach children different money lessons – saving, spending, donating, etc.
- It grows with the child – as the child's financial literacy matures, the money box is a way to introduce more complex concepts about money.
- It is a natural conversation starter in itself – when you hand over money to your child to keep in his money box, it is a teachable moment about how he will spend his money.

When you gift the money box to your child, be sure to explain its significance to him. Explain that if used wisely, the money box will be the key to their financial freedom in the future. You may need to explain what is meant by financial freedom, but it is unnecessary to explain any more beyond that. It is nice to have some mystery to the money box and let the children imagine what you mean by their money box being the key to their financial freedom. Another reason it is not necessary to explain any further at this point is because your future conversations with the children will contain many examples of how the lessons they learn from using money in the money box will be the key to their future financial freedom. The money in the money box, if used wisely, will give them choices later. Reinforce this concept in your future conversations with the children.

For older children, a money box may be a bit too childish though, I know of plenty of teenagers who love those cute little money boxes, even if they don't let on that they like them. If your child is too cool for a money box, a bank account may be an alternative, but I believe that a bank account is not the best way to teach a child (even an older child) about the concept of saving. This is because money in the bank is too abstract. A bank account involves the concept of money but if a child doesn't actually see the transaction or the cash, it is a difficult concept to teach. Children need to see and deal with money in a physical sense. It is difficult for them to understand money in the abstract - their brains just aren't mature enough.

... money in the bank is too abstract.

Keep in mind that a money box doesn't have to be a piggy bank. It can be something cool. For example, if your child likes mango smoothies from a particular juice bar, it is very easy to make a money box out of a take-away cup from the juice bar. You can go very fancy (I once watched a money box made out of a Starbucks cup on YouTube) or you can simply reuse the cup as a money box. Make sure your child drinks the smoothie first, before putting money into the cup!

Five money box features to consider

1. It works as a money box

We want to encourage our children to be comfortable around money. This means they should be exposed to money as often as possible and as young as possible. A child needs to be able to put money into the box and take it out to admire or count – all without the parent's help.

Parents are busy people. We don't want to have to take out the screwdriver to screw and unscrew the bottom of a money box on multiple occasions just because our child wants to see how much money he has saved (for the tenth time in the last hour). We just want a money box that is kid-friendly.

Money boxes that are opaque or ceramic or metal aren't useful. We want our children to be able to see the money inside those boxes to get a sense of achievement and pride in watching their money boxes fill up. If they can't see it, they won't be motivated. As the saying goes: Out of sight, out of mind.

We just want a money box that is kid-friendly.

2. It can be modified as the child's understanding about money matures

Cute-looking money boxes may delight very young children for a while. But as the child grows and preferences change, a cute mouse-shaped money box that he loved as a young child could become an embarrassment when he is a teenager. We don't want to have to buy a new money box each time he enters a new phase in his life.

Remember, when we gifted the first money box to our children, we emphasised its importance and significance. Replacing the money box constantly would contradict this message. We want the money box to be symbolic of their journey to financial freedom in the future. So we want a money box that can adapt to the child's preferences over time.

Money boxes with only one slot are practical to teach one money skill – saving. However, good money habits are more than just learning how to save. It's also learning to budget, which involves setting aside some money for different purposes. So we want a money box that can expand when our child is ready to progress with their learning.

3. It is durable

All young children are rough. They don't mean to be, but it is part of their development. Children will throw the money box around, drop it, roll it, step on it, sit on it, kick it – you name the action, they will do it.

A ceramic money box is shiny and cute, but it's also the most impractical money box to give to young children. It doesn't take much effort to break a ceramic money box. Most commercial plastic money boxes are also unsuitable because they are not durable – they crack easily when dropped. If you're going to buy a money box, look for one made of solid wood. Better yet, make your own to suit your child's temperament.

Ultimately, what we want is a money box that has significance and will withstand a child's rough treatment – after all, we expect the money box to last a child's lifetime!

4. It is simple to use – no bells, no whistles, no songs, no sound!

We don't want a counter display to tell our children how much money they have put into the box. We want our children to learn how to count money. In fact, one of the joys of earning money is actually counting the money itself and hearing that clink when a coin is dropped into the slot! We don't want some fancy noise played back when our children put coins into the money box.

Having sound or music played back is also irritating to the parents after a while. Yes, we want (in fact we should encourage) our children to take money out of their money box very often and count their progress; but we don't necessarily want the accompanying music each time they put their money back into the box. For the first few times it might amuse the child and encourage him to put money into the box, but over time, the sound will become just another background noise ... and the parents become increasingly irritated with the noise level in the home.

A moneybox with small slots that require our child to fold his notes multiple times just to get it into the money box isn't very practical. Over time, he will get frustrated with how much effort it takes to put money into and take money out of the moneybox and he will quickly lose interest.

5. It is good value

If we are going to teach our children about responsible spending and buying things of value, we want a money box that is of good value. This is not the same as cheap. There are plenty of cheap money boxes around that are not good value – they break easily, they don't function as money boxes or they are simply impractical.

The best money box is usually one that is made by you, your child, or both of you together. You know best what you want in a money box and you know best what lessons you want to use the money box for. It doesn't have to be fancy and it doesn't have to be bought – it just needs to fulfil *your* criteria of a money box. There is nothing wrong with using empty boxes, tins and other sturdy containers – in fact these may be the best type of money boxes because your child can personalise it by decorating it herself.

Use a bank account

Even though a bank account deals with money in the abstract, it is still important that all children have a savings account with a bank. In fact, I believe this is the first thing a parent should do when a child is born – open up a savings account (a baby won't appreciate a money box much at this age).

> ... put money into the account instead of buying gifts for your newborn baby.

Once you have opened up a bank account for your baby, well-intentioned relatives can then be asked to put money into the account instead of buying gifts for your newborn baby. Grandparents are usually pretty good with this type of suggestion. As the years go by, money for birthdays and Christmases, etc can all be deposited straight into the account. This is particularly useful if your child has generous relatives – you don't necessarily want your six year old to be handed $100 to put into his money box. You may prefer that this is deposited straight into the child's bank account.

For young children, the bank account is not a tool to teach money lessons but it is a necessity for when your child's money box is full and you need somewhere else to keep the money. When your child is mature enough to understand how a bank account works, you will need to explain to him where all that money goes to. Otherwise he will think all his hard work in earning and saving that money has simply disappeared. Depending on your child's understanding, it may even be time to introduce him to the concept of investing – earning interest in the bank. The bank is giving him money for simply having money in the bank account.

When your child understands how a bank account works, he will get very excited at the idea of the bank paying him interest for not doing any work at all. He will want to put his money in the bank very often. He might save $5 and ask for it to be put into the bank. Over time, this gets a bit tiring as the deposit request could come every few days. Multiply it by the number of children you have, and you'd be a very busy banker. To avoid this, decide when you want banking day to be. For my family, we have set the last day of each month as banking day. This is the day when the children empty out their savings box and hand their money over to me to take it to the bank. If you do electronic banking, you can do an online transfer and show your children the balance. You could also explain how electronic banking works, but for very young children this might be a wasted effort. Alternatively, if you have the time and are so inclined, it would be an exciting trip for the children to take their money to the bank themselves. If you can physically deposit your children's money into the bank, take them with you on the trip so they can see what a bank looks like. Be warned though there is a downside to this.

... decide when you want banking day to be.

I have taken David to the bank several times to deposit his money. He really enjoyed these trips because he gets to hand over his money for safe keeping and for his money to 'go to work'. One time, we walked past a branch of the bank. David asked, 'Is my money still in the bank?' I replied, 'Yep sure is. Safe and sound!'

David: Can we go in and have a look?
Me: Um … probably not because it's mixed with other people's money. But don't worry they keep a record of how much is yours.

David: Can I take it out?
Me (puzzled): Um … yes you can, but why would you?

David: Because I want to buy a mango smoothie.
Me: Well, once the money goes into the bank, the bank keeps it safe for you and you can't take it out until you're an adult. They do that in case you're tempted to take all your money out to buy junk food all the time. (Okay, I had to make this up on the spot because I couldn't think of anything else).

Ways to encourage saving

A habit is formed if an action is repeated many times. A habit is basically an auto-pilot. Research has shown it takes an average of 66 days for a new behaviour to become a habit. Of course some habits will take longer and some will take a shorter time to develop. But on the law of averages, let's work with 66 days. If we hand over pocket money once a week, that gives our children 52 weeks to form a habit. This is not going to be enough for two reasons. Firstly, it's only 52 times rather than the average 66 days. Secondly, the weekly ritual is only just that – weekly – rather than daily. So we're going to have to find other ways to encourage the saving habit in addition to using pocket money.

> If we hand over pocket money once a week, that gives our children 52 weeks to form a habit.

Other methods I have used to encourage my children to save include:

- Having rules about how much the children need to save

depending on the source of the money. For example, my six year old has to save half of his pocket money every week, but for birthdays and Christmas he has to save all of it.

- The children are given money from other sources. The tooth fairy is the most reliable source. From this, my children have to save at least half of what they get each time. They may choose to save more than half, but half is the minimum.
- Things they sell – all of my children have their own 'businesses' for items that they sell outside the home. Again they have to save a minimum of half of what they earn, but may choose to save all if they wish.
- Money from chores. Same rule – save half or save all.
- Asking my children to pay for the groceries or order takeaway food for me. They get to keep the loose change that comes back in the form of coins. Again, save at least half.

Once we supplement the weekly pocket money with other money transactions, there are plenty of opportunities for the children to practise the habit of saving money.

Make saving a family affair

There is a popular saying that 'more is caught than taught'. This is certainly true when it comes to parenting. Our children learn about saving from watching what we do. If we behave like spendthrifts, we can't expect our children to learn how to be a saver from our behaviour. We must model the habits we want our children to develop. This is not to say that if we want our children to learn to save, we can't spend on frivolous things. We all indulge sometimes, even those of us who are good with money. What we need to be careful of is the conversations we have with our children. Even frivolous spending has a place in conversation about saving money.

The habits we want to model for our children begin with our own self-reflection. We need to be honest with ourselves about our own natural tendencies. Are you a natural saver or a natural spender? Do you save or do you hoard? This self-reflection will help to either reinforce or change your money habits. If you are a natural spender but would like to cultivate a saving habit, tell your children this. You can even enlist their help to encourage you to become a saver by telling them what you are saving up towards. This could be new furniture, a new car, a family holiday, new shoes, whatever. Find ways to get your children to help you reach your goal.

> ... children understand there are things that mum and dad want but also have to save up for as well.

It's important we have conversations with our children about our own saving goals. We can talk about what we're doing to save and how we are tracking our saving progress. In this way, children understand there are things that mum and dad want but also have to save up for as well. They see delayed gratification at play and understand that when mum and dad impose limits on spending, the same rules apply to both adults and children.

I have a list of things I'd like to buy for our home. A lemon tree, a bag of seedling mix, a blueberry plant, muslin cloth for the plant, new spot lights for the kitchen, new carpets for the home, repaint the home, new kitchen, etc. I write this discretionary spending on a list and show it to the children. I then explained that I can't buy all of these things now and I will need to save. Some of these things (like a new kitchen) will take a few years of saving. Some of these things are for my own satisfaction (new carpets and new kitchen), while other things are for the family (lemon tree). As a family, we look through the list and decide on the next item we will save up towards. Recently, we picked the lemon tree. I explain that I am selling unused items around the home (such as the food processor, blender, etc), and our worm farm produce to help save up for the tree. Then I enlist my children's help by asking them if they would like to sell some of their unused toys. All proceeds go towards buying the lemon tree.

Saving for a family trip is a goal that the whole family can get involved in. Calculate the cost per person for the trip and draw up a savings chart. Place the chart in a prominent position so that the whole family – mum, dad and children – can see each other's progress and keep each other accountable.

There have been times when I have indulged despite having a goal to save towards. My children have questioned the indulgence (especially my natural saver). I take this as good feedback that my children have understood goal setting and the purpose of saving. Sometimes their questioning reminds me to set a good example for my children and refrain from spending while I am working towards a goal. Sometimes, I take this as an opportunity to have a conversation with my children that indulging from time to time is acceptable, as long as the indulgence doesn't become a habit. It's fine to spend on instant gratification from time to time.

Fun in tracking progress

Doing things for fun may not lead to a habit, but having fun makes it easier to learn new concepts. Find ways of making saving fun for your children.

One way I have engaged my children in a fun activity that also encourages saving is to create a visual chart of their progress.

Elisabeth loved colouring in pictures as a young child. When she was five years old, she desperately wanted a lady bug pillow. She begged me for it, but I wasn't too keen on buying her any more stuffed toys that she will lose interest in after a few weeks. So I wanted her to put in some effort into buying the pillow. I took her to the shops to find out how much it would cost to buy one. Then I made up a visual chart of letters that spell out 'LADY BUG PILLOW PET' in bubble writing. I asked Elisabeth to colour in a letter each time she saved 50 cents. When all the letters are coloured in, she will have enough to buy the pillow. It took her a while to save enough, but she didn't notice the length of time because she was engaged in the activity and had a lot of fun colouring in the letters. It was motivation for her to continue to save up her fifty cent coins.

> The important thing is to find out what is fun for your child and tailor the fun to the child.

I have successfully used this same exercise for subsequent savings goals for Elisabeth when she was younger. This doesn't quite work for my boys. Richard likes to count the money in his money box often so this counting serves as a reminder for him. David detests doing anything with pencils, crayons or any writing contraptions, so colouring in would not be much fun for him. The important thing is to find out what is fun for your child and tailor the fun to the child.

Fun in a bottle

At the time of writing this book, my family is trying out an activity. The rumour is that if a 600 mL Coca-Cola bottle is filled up to the top with $2 coins, it will have a total of $1000. We're going to give this a try, saving all of our $2 coins into an empty 600 mL Crystal Peak bottle.

It's a fun activity that can involve every family member. Every time we come across a $2 coin, we'd put it into the bottle. This fun activity has made us all more observant of the money that we spend. In particular, we are careful not to spend any $2 coins! As the coins fill the bottle, my children are taking turns at guessing how much is in there. It amazed my daughter that when the coins just covered the bottom of the bottle, there was already $30 saved up in the bottle!

I love this exercise because it can be used for any age group and for any purpose. For very young children who are learning about money in the abstract, this exercise can be used to develop his skills in recognising $2 coins. We can also use it to teach spatial awareness – the only gold coin that fits into the bottle is $2. For older children, this can be the savings 'jar' towards a big family trip at the end of the year. Much older children can use a bigger bottle to help them save for much bigger items – such as a phone or other electronic devices.

For very young children who are learning about money in the abstract, this exercise can be used to develop his skills in recognising $2 coins.

We plan to use the money in the bottle to pay for our family trip at the end of the year. At the time of writing, we have not filled the bottle, so I can't tell you how much money a 600 mL water bottle will hold. If you're interested in our progress, visit my blog page at Kids Money Habits (http://bit.ly/bottle-fun) for an update.

Rewarding progress

I used to think rewarding progress for long-term goals is the way to go. So far, I have found that implementing rewards hasn't worked out the way I thought it would. It's not the motivator or incentive that I thought would keep my children on track to save for longer term goals.

I started my children with short-term goals. Goals that they can achieve easily and the reward is in the end result itself. As they worked towards longer term goals, I implemented a reward system whereby they get to spend some of their saving on a treat once they achieve a set milestone. Their reaction when reaching their first milestone was a real eye-opener for me.

> They said they don't need to spend it on treats because they have fun saving up.

I encouraged my children to spend some of their savings on a treat by explaining that it wouldn't be much fun if all they do is save, save, save and don't reward themselves for their effort from time to time. They replied that if they used some of their savings on treats, then they'd have to save even longer! They would much prefer to put that money towards achieving their goal sooner. I don't quite agree with this reasoning because I can see it will lead to burnout when they are adults. I explained this to them. However, their next reasoning is what I would call a 'proud mama moment'. They said they don't need to spend it on treats because they have fun saving up. In other words, the journey itself is the reward. If this is their reward, then I don't need to worry about them burning out because they are already treating themselves along the way.

Summary

Young children who learn to set goals and strive to achieve those goals will continue to do so well into adulthood. Keeping it fun at this young age reinforces the process and encourages the children to continue to put aside some money for a future purpose. Over time, this behaviour will become a savings habit and you will have helped your children take another positive step in their lifetime journey to financial literacy.

Chapter 7
SPENDING

Introduction

We've done the hard work in cultivating our children's saving money habits. Now comes the fun part – spending that money! One reason we encourage our children to save money is so that they can eventually spend it. It wouldn't be much fun for them to save if they can't ever use that money for their own enjoyment.

The next important lesson for us to teach our children is wise spending. Be prepared – this is where children will make many mistakes with their money and it is where we need to give them some latitude, guidance and consolation. By cultivating good spending habits they will grow wiser about using their money.

This chapter explores the concept of what spending entails. It explains the difference between a want and a need based on the popular theory of Maslow's *Hierarchy of Needs*. This chapter then explains how we can set up a family system to guide our children to work out for themselves whether an item is something they want or something they need.

What is spending?

Spending isn't just using money wisely or unwisely. It's also not simply forking out money. When we donate money to charity, we're using money, but we don't associate this with spending. Spending is the exchange of money for something else. If we perceive this something else to be of equal or greater value than the money we have used, then we have spent our money wisely. Alternatively, if we perceive that something else to be of less value than the money we have used, then we feel short-changed. We are not satisfied that the item we received was worth the time, skill and effort we have given up – time, skill and effort we will never get back.

... the greater the amount spent, the greater the regret will be if the purchase turns out to be disappointing.

For children, whether the spending turns out to be wise or unwise can only be determined with hindsight. Unwise spending decisions have their foundation in regret – regret in paying a particular price for an item and whether that purchase lived up to our expectations. When we realise an item is not something we needed or even wanted, we regret buying it. Even if the item turned out to be a disappointment, most of us are unlikely to regret buying an item that costs only a few dollars: the amount isn't significant enough to worry us too much. However, the greater the amount spent, the greater the regret will be if the purchase turns out to be disappointing.

Children who are learning to spend money wisely will make many unwise purchases. They are not likely to have thought through their purchases much, nor will they have done enough research prior to their spending. We must gently point out their unwise decisions, explain to them why it was unwise and guide them to make wiser decisions in the future.

Spending is such a common habit ...

We can never entirely eliminate our purchasing regrets, but with experience and wisdom, the number of times we regret a purchase will diminish over time.

From a very young age, children see many examples of spending. Even babies observe their parents buying items on a regular basis. In fact, examples of spending arise in more instances than any other money concepts:

- Spending on groceries and treats
- Spending on birthday presents, Christmas presents and special occasions
- Spending on takeaway food and school lunch
- Spending on books and toys
- Spending on ... just about anything

Spending is such a common habit that a child really doesn't need any more encouragement to spend. The world is an encouragement. It is not surprising that one of the biggest money problems adults have is reining in their own spending.

While we don't need to teach our children to spend, we need to teach them how to spend wisely. Recall in Chapter 3 we explored the concept of earning being the exchange of our skill, time and effort for money. In Chapter 5 we explored the concept of saving being the delay in spending that money while we continue to earn money. Once we have earned and saved up enough money, spending is the next step. Spending is the exchange of that money for something else. Thinking of spending in this way makes us appreciate that when we spend, the money is gone, literally. We may be able to earn more money, but the time, skill and effort we gave up to earn the money in the first place is gone. We can't ever get back those times.

Why we should teach children about spending

If we don't step in and teach our children to spend wisely, a less ideal teacher will fill that role – the media or their equally clueless peers. Not too long ago, advertising was mainly on television, radio, newspapers, magazines and billboards. Today, advertising is much more widespread: YouTube, apps, movies, the internet, text messages, social media and even advergames. There is almost no limit when it comes to shameless advertising and product promotion.

There is almost no limit when it comes to shameless advertising and product promotion.

Here are some interesting facts about how children are affected by advertising (source: Raising Children Network: http://raisingchildren.net.au/articles/advertising.html):

- At 0-2 years, children can't tell the difference between advertising and actual programs
- At 3-6 years, children can tell the difference between advertising and actual programs, but do not understand that the advertisements are trying to sell something. Children are also not generally critical of the claims advertisers are making.
- At 7-11 years, children can see that the advertisements are trying to sell something, but do not always understand the products aren't as good as advertisements say they are, or that advertisers might not be telling them any of the bad points.
- At 12-13 years, children can use advertised information to decide what they want, but they may not understand how advertising makes things more expensive, or clever product placement strategies.

> ... the internet has made country-specific regulation increasingly ineffective.

Even though Australia has strict regulations about advertising directly to children under the age of 12 years old, the increasing connectedness of the world through the internet has made country-specific regulation increasingly ineffective. Further, many advertising regulations simply don't apply to advergames, which are increasingly being used by marketers to entice children into becoming familiar with and ultimately buying products. A child's buying decisions are affected by more than direct media influences such as advertising and the more subtle internet. Whilst we may be able to restrict our own children's exposure to marketing, we cannot limit the indirect influence of marketing through peer pressure. As our children mature in their perception of the world around them, they become increasingly aware of what their friends have that they don't have. If they have not already cultivated good money habits, peer influence is difficult to overcome.

One way to counter influence is by explaining to our children that each family has different priorities regarding how they spend their money. Our children and their friends have different priorities. By the time they are mature enough to observe and make comparisons with their peers, our children should be mature enough to understand that the more they spend on things they want (or think they want), the quicker they will run out of money. This in turn means having to work longer to replace the money or worse still, borrowing to finance things that they want. Allowing our children to make unwise spending decisions in these early years will improve their spending decisions over time and will ultimately cultivate their good spending habits.

... our children should be mature enough to understand that the more they spend on things they want (or think they want), the quicker they will run out of money.

Wants vs Needs: Concept

We teach our children to spend wisely by teaching them to spend on things that are of good value. One way to teach them good value is to teach them the difference between wanting something and needing something.

At its simplest and most basic, children should be taught to spend their money on things they need. This is tricky for young children, because they are not able to fully comprehend what they need. Having guiding principles for the family is good for young children to follow, until they are mature enough to fully understand the difference between 'wants' and 'needs'. Many adults struggle with precisely defining what they want and what they need, so we will have to give our children a lot of guidance in this area.

Many adults struggle with precisely defining what they want and what they need, so we will have to give our children a lot of guidance in this area.

One of the most powerful videos I have shown my children to start our journey about 'wants' and 'needs' is from The *Story of Stuff* (http://storyofstuff.org). From these videos my children gained an understanding of what their stuff is doing to the planet and to the people around them. It started a conversation in our household about 'wants' and 'needs'. It's very easy to ask children to list items they want and items they need. But wants and needs exist on a spectrum with 'want' on one end and 'need' at the other end. For example, everyone needs food and shelter but chocolates and lollies are treats that many people want. These general descriptions are good examples to use when teaching children a high-level concept, to get children thinking about the difference between something they want and something they need. Drill down to the details and it becomes more difficult to classify an item into something we 'want' and something we 'need. Take soft drinks as an example. While most of us don't need the sugary fizzy soft drink, diabetics with low blood sugar levels sometimes need to have access to sugar to help control their sugar level. To diabetics, soft drinks containing sugar may sometimes be a need.

If your child is old enough, explain Maslow's *Hierarchy of Needs* (http://bit.ly/2vAA972).

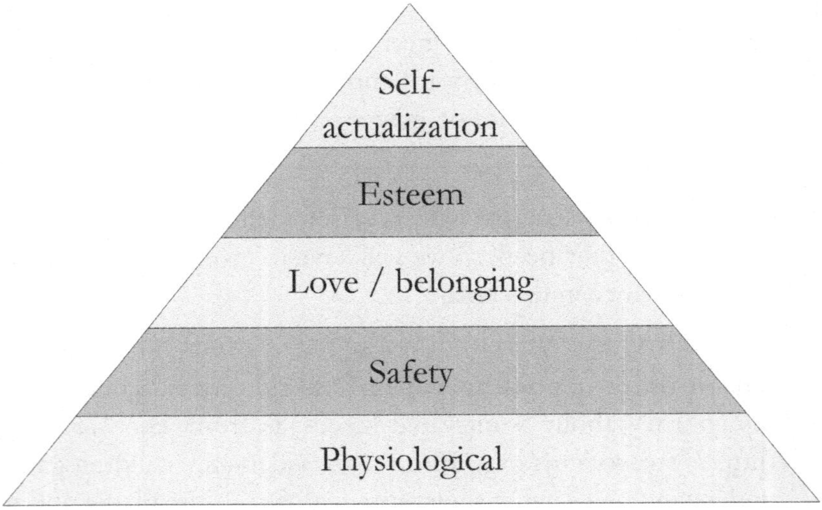

I cannot do justice to Abraham Maslow by explaining his *Hierarchy of Needs* in detail. For those who wish to gain a deeper understanding, there are many good books or even the internet that can explain his concepts better than I can. However, a brief explanation of the *Hierarchy of Needs* in this chapter may be helpful. The theory behind this hierarchy is that a person will behave in ways to satisfy her lower level needs first before she can behave in ways to satisfy the higher level needs. Therefore, to understand a person's behaviour, we must identify the need that the behaviour is seeking to fulfil. Only once a lower level need is satisfied can this person behave in ways to satisfy a higher level need. Here is a simple explanation of the five levels of needs from Simply Psychology (http://bit.ly/2w1VLwy).

Maslow's *Hierarchy of Needs*	
Self-actualisation needs	Realising personal potential, self-fulfillment, seeking personal growth and peak experiences.
Esteem needs	Achievement, mastery, independence, status, dominance, prestige, self-respect, respect from others.
Love or belonging needs	Friendship, intimacy, trust and acceptance, receiving and giving affection and love. Affiliating, being part of a group (family, friends, work).
Safety needs	Protection from elements, security, order, law, stability, freedom from fear.
Biological and physiological needs	Air, food, drink, shelter, warmth, sex, sleep.

If an item is on the lower two Maslow levels – biological, physiological and safety – it's easy to decide whether the item is a 'want' or a 'need'. For example, it is not disputed that items which satisfy our biological and physiological needs fall into the 'need' category – we need food, water, air. Similarly, items that satisfy our safety needs also fall into the 'need' category – we need to obey the law and wear a helmet when riding a bicycle to be safe.

But as we move up the hierarchy it becomes more difficult. When it comes to love or belonging, esteem and self-actualisation, it becomes more difficult to classify something as a 'want' or a 'need'. Many teenagers will argue for their need to belong with their friendship groups and justify having the latest gadgets as something they need in order to belong to that friendship group, or to help with their own self-esteem.

> These principles are where your family's values, attitudes and beliefs about money and other moral and ethical beliefs will come together.

This is why it's important to have guiding principles for the family. It's important to allow these principles to evolve over time as and when each family member's social environment changes. Family guiding principles vary between families. These principles are where your family's values, attitudes and beliefs about money and other moral and ethical beliefs will come together.

I often refer back to the *Story of Stuff* in money conversations with my children regarding wants and needs. We often talk about the impact it would have if we simply bought the things we needed rather than things we wanted. We talk about what is really causing the planet to deteriorate – is it the making of 'wants' or the making of 'needs' that causes the problem? We inevitably come to the conclusion that most 'needs' are compatible with the environment whereas it's the 'wants' that causes a lot of the problems for the environment. The pollution from factories that makes stuff people want releases toxic gas into the environment. Due to plastic compounds, most plastic toys are not recyclable. Many children's toys are not made to last and break only after a few hours of use. As these are not recyclable, the broken toys are thrown into the rubbish bin, which goes to landfill. The stuff we send to landfill is not easily broken down because they are often not made from natural resources. Even when things eventually break down, toxic chemicals leach into the soil and ground water. These eventually find their way to the seas causing problems to sea life as well.

In a conversation with your children, come up with guiding principles on how to work out whether something is a 'need' or a 'want'. These principles should be ones that your family can apply when contemplating a purchase. Test the principles against a few items around the home and continue to refine the principles until you finally reach a stage where the principles work most of the time. When you have these guiding principles, write them down and display them in a prominent place at home to serve as a reminder to everyone.

... come up with guiding principles on how to work out whether something is a 'need' or a 'want'.

Guiding principle conversation – a personal example

The guiding principles that my family have come up with to distinguish something we want from something we need is an evolving one. It started when I was hanging out the laundry and Richard (then eight years old) was helping me. In casual conversation, I asked him how he works out whether something is a 'want' or a 'need'.

Richard: A need is something that if you don't have it, you'll die. Things like food and shelter.

Me: What about clothes? Is that a need?
Richard: Yes, it keeps us warm.

Me: So in summer months, clothes are no longer a need?
Richard: Well, you still need to wear something to protect your skin.

Me: Cavemen didn't have clothes like T-shirts or shorts.
Richard: But we have to wear clothes otherwise we'd go nudie and that would be breaking the law.

Me: So one way of working out if something is a want or a need is if we didn't have the thing, it would be breaking the law.
Richard: Yep.

[To test this guideline, I asked further]
Me: What about school uniforms (I happened to be pegging the children's school uniforms). Is that a need or a want?
Richard: That's a need because it tells everyone which school we go to. It's the school rules.

[This is me challenging his thinking a bit more]
Me: If your circle of friends say that to belong in that friendship group, the rule is that everyone must have an iPhone, does the iPhone become a need?
Richard: No.

Me: What's the difference between a school saying you need to wear a uniform and a circle of friends saying you need an iPhone?
Richard: Maybe I don't need a school uniform – but if I don't wear one, I'd get into trouble.

Me: I think the difference is that the law says you need to go to school and whichever school you go attend you have to follow

> the rules of the school. One of these rules is wearing the school uniform. So when you're wearing a school uniform, it is linked back to the law. There is no law that says you have to be with a particular circle of friends so when you don't have an iPhone you're not breaking any law.
>
> So my family's guidelines on defining whether something is a want or a need are as follows. Something is a need if:
> - We will die or be seriously injured if we don't have it.
> - We're breaking the law (either directly or indirectly) if we don't have it.

This list will inevitably grow as and when I have more of these conversations with other family members. It will also change as the children's social situations change. As my children's understanding matures, I intend to expand this definition to include an explanation for needing things that will maintain or enhance their quality of life. This is essentially Maslow's fifth level of needs.

Is it a need – how to really tell

People are creatures of comfort. We think we need a lot of things to live comfortably, but it would surprise many of us how little we actually need. Growing up, I often heard my mother say that life is very simple and people don't need a lot to live comfortably. I am passing these words of wisdom down to my children and showing them that life can in fact be lived very simply.

Go camping!

Camping is a fun outdoor activity for the whole family and many families are now using this as a way to pry their children away from electronics (though I often see children at campsites playing on their electronic devices). My family enjoy going camping. It is our escape from the busy city life that we lead and it's an open space for the children to run and explore and be wild. What I love most about camping is the night time. There is a certain meditative feel to sitting in the darkness, lit only by the camp fire and surrounded by nature. Toasting marshmallows and watching with amusement as the children debate how to keep the fire alive without any of them braving the dark to collect more firewood.

My husband often points out the constellations to the children. They now recognise the Southern Cross, the Milky Way, Orion's belt, Mercury and Jupiter amongst many of the wonders in the night sky. One time, I saw my first shooting star at a campsite and the children asked me to make a wish. I remember thinking there was nothing else I would wish for – everything I loved was there with me that night.

Going camping also has the added benefit of teaching the children how little we actually need in our lives. A friend told me how his camping trips remind him that life can be simple. He is a bushwalking enthusiast and compared to the trips my family makes, he would be considered a hard-core camper. My family transports our camping gear to the campsite by car and then sets up. My friend carries everything he needs in a rucksack and walks to the campsite. So while I cleaned my dishes with detergent, sponge and water, he would do the same with soil and rinse with water away from the creek. For me, a sponge and detergent are items I need but for him, they are simply not worth carrying.

As my family become more experienced campers (and as the children grow older), we are likely to cut back on the mod cons that we bring to our camping trips. There's nothing as satisfying as knowing that we managed a few days in the bush with just the basics. Going bush also puts things into perspective and shows us what is really important in life. For the children, it's not much fun at campsites if they didn't have siblings to play with, so they learn to appreciate each other a lot more. It's also not much fun if they didn't have friends to play with, so camping encourages them to make new friends. I also learned to relax my standards of cleanliness and germs.

We're also more grateful for our cosy little home and warm bed when we return from our camping trips. The convenience of a flush toilet that is just outside our bedroom, running water to wash anything and the microwave to heat our breakfast are all things we take for granted.

Going bush also puts things into perspective and shows us what is really important in life.

Watch movies

My daughter and I have started to watch the *Little House on the Prairie* series. She was amazed at how simple life was back in those days.

There were no toys in sight, no electricity, televisions, radios or telephones (much less an iPhone)! Children's time was occupied by doing chores, their homework or playing outside. There were no cars. Children walked everywhere. (Today, lack of exercise is one reason why obesity is a problem.) Things had multiple uses. The same building was used as a school on weekdays and as a church on weekends. The children didn't have many clothes to wear and would often wear the same set of clothes again in the same week.

Whilst this is only a television series, there is much truth in how simply people can live. The way we choose to live today is luxurious compared with how life was back then. This begs the question – if people were able to live simply many generations ago, why can't we?

Watching these television series and other movies about those less fortunate has altered the way my children see their own world. We often talk about the poor children in African countries who don't have much, but I get the feeling that for some of my children, this is just another story, no different to fairy tales that we read to them every night. But movies and television series somehow make it more real for the children. When we watch movies such as *A Little Princess* or *The Pursuit of Happiness* the children have often reflected on what they have – their toys, comfort, family, home, opportunities. They develop a gratitude for the life that they have.

Lessons on spending

Once our children have decided that an item is something they need (or even want), we then teach them how to satisfy that need – that is, teach them how to spend their money wisely.

> The only way to become wise is to practise.

We all want our children to eventually learn to make wise decisions when spending their money. The only way to become wise is to practise. Many unwise decisions must be made before the children will eventually learn to make wise decisions.

When the children are young, they don't spend much money, so unwise decisions they make with their money don't have a significant effect. It is better that they are allowed to make unwise decisions and learn their lessons when they are young than when they are grown up, where money mistakes can sometimes be very costly. Avoid using words such as 'good' or 'bad' and instead use words such as 'wise' or 'unwise'. 'Good' and 'bad' are words people use to describe the quality or character of something or someone, whereas 'wise' and 'unwise' implies a learning process.

Develop a few simple spending guidelines for the children to follow until they learn to distinguish between wise and unwise decisions. The following are some guidelines I have for my children.

Quality, not cost

Buying the cheapest item isn't always the wisest spending decision because many cheap items don't last a long time. Similarly, paying more for an expensive item doesn't always mean it's a better product. Many cheap items function just as well as the more expensive version. Because we value our money, we ought to spend our money on items of value to us, rather than be dictated by the price of the item. I often use food to explain the concept of value to the children. We need food to survive. Junk food, fresh fruits and vegetables are all examples of food. When we feel hungry, we can buy junk food, fresh fruits or vegetables to satisfy that hunger. Junk food usually costs less to buy than healthy food. A study done by Cambridge University in 2012 found that it costs three times more to fill the same number of calories with healthy food compared with filling the same number of calories with junk food. But we know it would be unwise to spend money on chips and chocolates, rather than on fresh fruits and vegetables to fill that hunger. Junk food isn't quality food and the longer term effect on our health makes it a more costly alternative to healthy food.

I also use meat as an example. Our local shop sells meat of varying quality, marked by the star rating on each tray of meat. A higher star rating represents a better quality of meat. The approximate costs of these are: two-star meat tray $5, three-star tray $9, four-star tray $11 and five-star tray $15. All trays weigh the same and the only difference is the quality of the meat. I explain to the children that if the grocery budget was tight, I'd have to buy the two-star tray of meat for $5 but that wouldn't be as good for our health as a tray with higher-rated stars. A four- or five-star tray of meat is more expensive, but if budget permits, I would prefer to pay more for a better quality meat because it's better for our health.

Things that can be replenished

Spending on items that can be replenished naturally is a more sensible choice than spending on items that must be manufactured. The *Story of Stuff* is again referred to in many of my money conversations with the children regarding spending on things that are environmentally sustainable. If we only bought things we need, it would be better for the environment.

However, sometimes things that are environmentally friendly can be more expensive than things that are toxic to the environment. For example, using plastic to make a money box is more toxic to the environment, given the chemicals that are used to make plastic.

In comparison a money box made of wood is better for the environment but would often be more expensive to buy as it more labour-intensive and cannot be mass-produced quickly. Despite an environmentally friendlier product being more expensive initially, in the long term, it is invariably the better option than one made to be replaced. Constantly replacing a product that was not made to last can mean what was otherwise a less expensive product becomes more expensive in the long term.

Constantly replacing a product that was not made to last can mean what was otherwise a less expensive product becomes more expensive in the long term.

Sometimes being environmentally friendly is also compatible with spending less money. For example, it's more convenient to buy a bottle of lemonade than it is to buy the lemons to make lemonade. But the bottle of lemonade requires the plastic bottle to be manufactured whereas the lemons are simply plucked from a lemon tree. Lemons are easily composted with little use of energy compared to recycling a bottle. Buying the lemons is therefore a more sensible spending decision than buying a bottle of lemonade because the lemons can be replenished naturally. The cost of lemons and sugar are usually less than the cost of a bottle of lemonade, and would be even less if you or a neighbour has a lemon tree to give you free lemons. This has the added bonus that you know exactly what is in your drink.

Another example is play dough. The plastic pots of play dough from the shops are toxic – and the manufactured pots ultimately end up in landfill. Home-made play dough is simply flour that can be washed away. Home-made play dough may or may not be cheaper than the plastic pot version because the home-made version doesn't have a long shelf-life so you will need to make a batch more frequently than the plastic pot version.

Special occasions

Children these days have been indoctrinated into thinking they should buy something special for Mothers' Day, Fathers' Day, birthdays, Christmas, Easter, Valentine's Day, etc. They believe the way to make the recipient feel special is by showering the recipient with chocolates, flowers, gifts, etc.

It's not only children who have been influenced by the media in this regard. Parents too, have been conditioned into thinking that the only acceptable present to buy our children on their birthday is toys. If Harry likes Star Wars Lego, then I will buy Harry some Star Wars Lego. Grandma will do the same, as will aunties and uncles. It doesn't matter that Harry's toy box is already overflowing with Star Wars Legos because buying another box will make Harry happy. Harry therefore ends up with at least four boxes of Star Wars Lego – from the parents, aunty, uncle and grandparents. How many will he end up using? Probably none, since he doesn't need any more Star Wars Legos. Incidentally, Lego pieces cannot be recycled.

Many of us know it is not the gift that is appreciated. We have all heard that money can't buy happiness and that it is the gesture that is appreciated, rather than the gifts themselves. The gifts are what marketers have told us is a symbol of love. Truly demonstrating love is best done through thoughts rather than the things that are given. When understood in this way, there is really no need to feel obliged to spend anything on special occasions. Yet we can't help ourselves. We have been conditioned into thinking that we have to bring a present to a party as a courtesy. Many of us are uncomfortable to turn up empty-handed, even if the host says not to bring anything. I am still working on being comfortable with empty hands.

If we really want to give a present, it is the thoughtful presents that mean a lot more than boxes of chocolates and flowers. An apron that mum needs in the kitchen means a lot more than an expensive necklace, especially if mum already wears her favourite necklace every day. Putting more thought into what the other person will appreciate or need shows genuine effort. Instead of succumbing into buying birthday cards, why not make one from the heart? Instead of buying a cake, why not make one from the kitchen at home? The home-made cake may not look as good, but sure tastes better than a cake that was not made with love.

> ... we should never use money *only* to make people feel special – friendship and love cannot be bought.

Special occasions are timely reminders for us to talk to our children about expressing our feelings for each other all the time. We don't need a day set aside for us to tell each other how much we love each other and to show our appreciation every day rather than on that specific day.

I teach my children that we should never use money *only* to make people feel special – friendship and love cannot be bought. Making people feel special should come from the heart, not from the gifts we give.

No more presents in our household

In our household, we have stopped buying birthday presents for our children. It started when I was fed up with the insane number of toys that my older two children got from their grandparents on their birthdays and Christmas. I didn't want to add to any more of the stuff, so I started giving my children coupon books for their birthdays every year. The value of the coupon books themselves are worth more than the price of any toys I would buy for them.

The coupons entitle the birthday child to things like:

- Baking time
- Day out with daddy
- Day out with mummy
- Breakfast of my choice
- Responsibility-free day
- Special drink at the café, etc.

When my youngest was old enough to realise what the coupon book was, he started asking for one for his birthday as well. On several occasions, I have asked my children whether they want toys for their birthday instead of a coupon book and unanimously they say they prefer coupon books.

To me, that's a win-win all around.

- It's a win for me because I no longer need to spend much time thinking what to give them for a present.
- It's a win for them because it gives them special occasions with mum and/or dad whenever they use the coupons.
- It's a win for the environment because the coupon books are simply pieces of recycled paper.
- It's a win for the family because we get to do things together as a family when the child uses the family-related coupons.

I am now receiving coupon books from my children for my birthday and for Mothers' Day. They are simple lovely gestures such as:

- One car wash
- Breakfast in bed
- One cup of coffee
- Fruit salad and juice for breakfast
- Morning time with Elisabeth, Richard or David
- Afternoon time with Elisabeth, Richard or David

Buying things you don't need

When children start to understand the concept of comparison pricing, they will inevitably fall into the trap of thinking that they should buy things when the items are discounted. They start identifying 'bargains'. This is an opportunity to have a conversation with them that a bargain is not a bargain if they are buying things they don't need.

When a bargain is not a bargain

One time while watching the television, Richard was intrigued by an infomercial about a particular type of paint roller. He was glued to the TV for the whole infomercial and then copied down the telephone number to ring at the end. He handed me the piece of paper and told me to ring the number to buy this really cool paint roller. It was only $14.95 and it would minimise mess when painting. There would also be less paint wasted as everything is stored inside the roller. This would have been a brilliant idea, except we don't paint. So despite the roller being only $14.95 it wasn't a bargain because we don't need it. The roller was actually three instalments of $14.95 plus postage and handling – no longer a bargain.

Spend some, save some

The concept of 'future' is lost on young children. Many young children live in the day – and this is not something we want to change. We don't want overly fretful and anxious children who worry so much about tomorrow that they forget to enjoy today.

Expressing time as present and future doesn't have the same meaning for children as they do for adults. Technically, the future is any time that is yet to come. (The future never comes; only the present does.) However, when adults refer to the future, it is commonly understood as a point in time at least five to ten years from now (according to the adults I have asked). For children however (especially the younger ones) their future is the next day!

When teaching children to save, it's better to use more concrete examples. Instead of saying 'Save some of your money to spend in the future' I would often say 'Save some of your money towards the home that you might buy when you're an adult.' For many parents, the idea of telling their child to save for a home they might buy as adults seems absurd, especially if their child is only six years old. You don't have to use a home as an example of something your child spends their money on in the future. It can be anything that costs a lot of money and take a long time to save up towards. I used the home as an example with my children because I have so many money conversations with my children and the idea of them saving up to buy their home is simply one of these conversations. All of my children understand that one million is a larger number than one hundred thousand (yes, including my six year old – he loves maths). They may not yet appreciate what it really means, but at least they know the former is a much larger number than the latter. I have shown my children the price of houses and apartments in the area we live so they understand how much money people need in order to buy a home in the suburb we live in. I would also use this as an example to teach my children about reasons why people borrow money from the bank. Remember, money conversations are not guided by the age of our children, but by their financial maturity and understanding.

> I would also use this as an example to teach my children about reasons why people borrow money from the bank.

Bigger isn't always better

We can easily fall into the trap of thinking that bigger represents better value. This isn't always true.

An example I have used with my own children is the size of our home. I used to think that we will need to move into a bigger home as the children grow bigger. After some reflection, I realised that I would prefer the children to spend more time outdoors in the fresh air and to work off all that energy. A bigger home may have a bigger internal living area, but many inner-city homes in Sydney do not offer the spacious outdoors that growing children need. Houses around my suburb are classic old terraces, with not a lot of space inside or outside the house. Older children are also likely to engage in more extra-curricular activities, hanging out with friends or working at a job, which means they are not likely to be home all that much. So as the children grow bigger, it might seem intuitive to move into a bigger home, but when we think about how much time we actually spend in the home, it seems counter-intuitive to buy a bigger home when we won't be home that often. A bigger home also means more cleaning and it's not something any of us want to be spending much of our time doing.

In any case, more often than not, an existing home becomes bigger once we de-clutter and minimise the stuff we have inside the home.

Waiting to spend

Depending on your child's maturity, some parents have success in implementing a one-week rule: when your child wants something, ask her to write down what it is, where she saw it and how much it was. Then ask her to wait a week to think it over. If she still wants the item after a week, she can work to pay for half the amount of the item. If she is willing to wait and then work for it, she must really want the item. But if she protests or doesn't want to wait, she probably doesn't covet the item as much as we thought.

If she is willing to wait and then work for it, she must really want the item. But if she protests or doesn't want to wait, she probably doesn't covet the item as much as we thought.

When Elisabeth wanted a lady bug pillow pet, she knew I would ask her to pay for it herself. From our previous conversations, she knew that if she waited long enough, the shop will discount the item to get stock moving. So she waited and waited and waited. She often went back to visit that shop every time we went to the shopping centre, just to check if her favourite pillow pet is still there but more importantly, to check on the price. After three months of waiting and checking, Elisabeth came to me one day we were at the shops and begged me to allow her to buy the lady bug pillow (she didn't bring her money on that trip and needed to borrow from me). I resisted. She then launched into her debating mode (I wasn't surprised when she made it into the school debating team several years later, in Year 5).

Reasons why she should buy the lady bug pillow now: It was $12 when she first saw it and she's been checking the price every week for almost three months and has seen the price slowly decline. She's just checked it again and it is now $6. Can she pleeease buy it now? I asked coyly, 'Why don't you wait longer and the price might go down even further?' I saw her face change from one of hope and anticipation to one that is about to blow up with exasperation. 'It might be sold out by then, or the shops might take them all off the shelf – there are only a few left!' I always appreciate good debating, so I handed over $6 to Elisabeth. She immediately reimbursed me the money when we got home.

So after months of waiting, Elisabeth was finally rewarded for her patience. She bought her beloved lady bug pillow pet for half the original price. She had saved up the full price for the pillow pet, but because she was patient in buying it, not only did she end up with a pillow pet, she had change to spare! Apart from the saving aspect, Elisabeth also learnt that the gratification she got from delaying her purchase was so much greater than if she had bought it when she wanted it. The anticipation itself made the reward so much sweeter. I believe this was the turning point in my five year old Elisabeth learning about the rewards of delayed gratification.

> ... the gratification she got from delaying her purchase was so much greater than if she had bought it when she wanted it.

Multi-purpose items may be better

In a world of abundance, there's a gadget for nearly everything. We have grown accustomed into thinking that unless we have a specific item for a specific task, we simply can't get things done. Over time, we have lost the ability to imagine multiple uses for the same item. Using an item for multiple purposes minimises purchases, and having less things frees up space, with the latter especially applicable in small homes, where space is at a premium.

This is where having a minimalist mentality will serve us well. There is no definition of what a minimalist is, but the core of minimalism is to keep only items that serve a purpose which cannot be served by anything else. Minimalism is a journey in itself.

I haven't always been a minimalist and embarked on that journey about seven years ago when I decided I no longer want to be a slave to working until I reached old age. So when things around my household break, rather than replacing those items immediately, I gave considerable thought to whether the functions of the broken item can be served by existing items we already had around the home. More often than not, I am astounded by how creative I become.

> I haven't always been a minimalist and embarked on that journey about seven years ago when I decided I no longer want to be a slave to working until I reached old age.

One household item, multiple uses

A good example to explain minimalism is our kettle. For years we had an electric kettle, and when it stopped working, I instinctively started browsing catalogues for a new kettle. But then I thought about how people used to boil water before the invention of kettles. Five years since our kettle stopped working and we still haven't bought a replacement. We now boil our water in a saucepan. It is the same saucepan we often used to boil eggs and stew apples.

Another household item we don't buy for our household is drinking glass. Young children are prone to dropping their glass. When my children grew out of drinking from plastic cups, instead of buying ceramic cups or drinking glass, I simply gave them empty jam jars to use as drinking vessels. We have been using empty jam jars long before it became a trend at fancy restaurants. If the children accidentally knock one off the table and shatter the glass, we simply scoop up the glass and put it into the recycling bin. We take another glass jar out of the cupboard as replacement. The same glass jars are used for serving soup, milk shakes, milk. They are also used for storing baking supplies such as sugar, desiccated coconut, chocolate chips, almonds, home-made jams, etc. At one point we also used the jars as money boxes.

> ... what else we can use around the home to serve that purpose.

So before we buy a replacement item, we think about what else we can use around the home to serve that purpose. If we conclude we need to buy a replacement, look for one that can be used for multiple purposes.

Summary

Places where we can spend our money are endless. There is no shortage of people wanting our money, so we need to be wise with our money decisions. Wisdom comes with age and experience, both of which young children lack. So we allow our young children to make many small unwise decisions with their money and in that process, gently guide them towards making wiser ones. In theory, young children's unwise spending decisions shouldn't be costly. However, the lines of products that are marketed to children and those marketed to adults are becoming blurred. One consequence of this is that young children's spending decisions can sometimes be a major blunder, like in-app purchases. When we foresee this, we should protect them from the major blunders rather than allow them to make the unwise spending decision.

While children are gaining their wisdom with money, having family guidelines for young children to follow is often very helpful to clarify the family's values, attitudes and beliefs about how money is to be used.

Wisdom comes with experience and experience comes from making many unwise decisions.

Chapter 8
SPENDING IN PRACTICE

Introduction

No matter how hard our children work to earn money and no matter how much they save, if they do not spend their money wisely, their money will soon be frittered away. Good spending habits are perhaps the most challenging habit to cultivate in children. As with any other habits, it takes an average of 66 days for a new behaviour to become a habit. There are additional challenges with cultivating spending habits. Good spending habits come with wisdom which takes time and can only be cultivated after making unwise decisions.

We are programmed to protect our children and allowing our children to make unwise decisions in life is heart-wrenching. It is difficult for us to stand by and watch our young children make unwise decisions with their hard-earned money. Yet instinctively we know the importance of allowing our children to learn through making unwise decisions because this is one way to develop wisdom. Once they know about what not to do they should learn about what to do, and hence learn about both.

This chapter explores the different ways and opportunities for children to make real life decisions with money within a controlled environment and under our guidance and wisdom. The more our children practise making decisions with money, the more wisdom they will accumulate.

Ways to teach children wise spending

1 | Go shopping

One of the best opportunities to teach children about spending is by going shopping. That's right, take them shopping! But it's not what you think. I'm referring to taking them to do the grocery shopping. Why grocery shopping? Children are less tempted by food than by toys. This is not to say there is no temptation with junk food, but it's at least not as expensive if you decide to give in to their temptation and it doesn't clutter up the home.

> Children are less tempted by food than by toys.

There are so many lessons we can teach our children when we go shopping and best of all, it happens frequently. If your family goes grocery shopping every week, the opportunity to teach arises every week, either refining what we teach or adding to our earlier lessons.

What lessons can we teach our children when we take them to shop for groceries?

Lesson 1 – the labels on shelves aren't what they seem to be

There are so many 'special' labels on the shelves that it can become very confusing. There are labels to tell us which items are discounted for the week only, labels to tell us which items are being discontinued, labels to tell us which items are discounted because it is close to their use-by date and labels to tell us which items have had their prices reduced permanently. If we are not careful in identifying the labels, we could be mistaken into believing that everything in the store is a good bargain.

Pointing out to the children the different labels used by shops for different purposes helps them understand that not all labels are a bargain and it is important to read the labels themselves to be familiar with the different ones used in the store.

> ... not all labels are a bargain ...

Lesson 2 – comparison spending

Comparison spending has two different meanings:

- Comparing the costs of two or more different products (unit pricing or usage pricing).
- Comparing the amount spent at two different points in time (spending budget comparison).

Unit pricing

Unit pricing comparison is best taught when children understand the concept of 'bigger and smaller', for example, that 100 is a bigger number than 10. Remember, it is not our children's age but rather their level of financial literacy and maturity that guides what we teach them and when.

When comparing prices of different sized products, it can be misleading if we simply looked at the price tag. I once showed David a 200 gram packet of chips which costs $2.00 and a 250 gram packet of chips that costs $2.40. Both were the same type of chips and flavour and the only difference was the size of the packet. I asked him to choose the packet he thought was better value. He chose the 200 gram packet – because it costs less. This is a very common misunderstanding for young children, and even some adults.

While the lighter packet may appear cheaper than a heavier packet of chips, when we're comparing products of different sizes, we have to work out how much the product costs per unit of measurement. Here, the unit of measurement is grams.

Cost [$]	Weight [grams]	Calculation	Cost per 100 grams
2.00	200	($2.00/200) x 100	$1.00
2.40	250	($2.40/250) x 100	$0.96

On a per gram basis, the heavier packet works out to be cheaper. In Australia, price tags of products on shelves must display the price per unit of measurement, so I showed David how to read the labels on the shelf to compare the prices using a common measurement metric.

Usage pricing

As if unit pricing is not tricky enough, sometimes using the weight of the product as a base for comparing can be misleading. So while shops are legally required to display price per unit, those unit prices may be nonsensical when we consider how the product is consumed. It is sometimes more accurate to work out the cost per use of the item than the cost per weight of the item. Big products of individually packed items are the perfect example where weight comparison is very misleading.

For example, consider the following:

	Price [$]	Number of items	Weight [grams]	Cost per 100 grams	Cost per item
Product A	5.00	10	300	$1.67	$0.50
Product B	7.00	15	400	$1.75	$0.46

If we used the weight of the products as a base unit for comparison we would decide to buy product A because it's cheaper. But these products are consumed as individual items rather than by weight. So product A has 10 serves and product B has 15 serves. To work out which one is really cheaper, it is more accurate to calculate the unit pricing according to how the contents are used up. Calculating the unit price according to the number of items in each product tells us that product B costs less per item – each time we use one item in product A it costs 50 cents, and for product B it is 46 cents.

Having explained unit pricing and usage pricing, it is also a fine line that we walk to teach the children that sometimes, buying the larger unit may be unwise spending, even if it works out to be cheaper on a unit or usage basis. This is because if we don't use all of what we have bought and some of it is thrown away, we have effectively thrown away some of our money. For example, if we only want a small carton of milk, buying a 2 litre bottle of milk won't be good value if it means the rest of the contents will not be drunk and will be thrown away.

Spending budget comparison

I get really excited when I do spending budget comparison with my children. This is probably the accountant in me coming to the surface – I love playing with spreadsheets! This exercise involves comparing the amount we spent on a particular trip this year with the amount spent on the same trip last year. If there is a holiday trip that your family takes every year (e.g., skiing trip, camping trip, amusement park, interstate or overseas holiday), this is an activity that can really open up many money lessons and, in particular, spending lessons. It can also tap into your children's creativity about how to spend less.

At the end of the trip, I add up all the costs of the trip. I mean all of the costs – entry tickets, car hire, petrol, food, necessities and treats, extra spending, equipment hire – everything! I then compare the total with what we spent last year. If we spent less, we work out what we did differently this year compared to last year. Then we celebrate by putting that extra we 'saved' this year towards a family saving goal. On the other hand, if we spent more, we drill down on why we spent more – was it because we added a few more activities in this year's trip? Did we go for an extra day longer? Did we buy more 'wants' this year compared to last year? We look through the different categories where we spent money (food, clothing, treats, etc) and work out why the trip costs more this year.

It's best to start with the biggest expenditures – usually accommodation and transport – and work out if there are cheaper alternatives for next year. Family trips cost a lot of money, so when we find alternative ways to have the same trip, the savings can be very rewarding. One year we found that simply changing the accommodation halved the cost of our entire trip the following year!

Lesson 3 - Know the price and value of everything

Encouraging our children to look at the shopping list teaches them what can be bought for the same amount of money. It also teaches them the concept of value and how to work out priorities when the budget is tight.

I once asked Elisabeth (then 11 years old) to look through the supermarket receipt and identify the most expensive item. She exclaimed that the 500 gram tray of minced meat was more expensive than a set of camping mats that we bought for our camping trip! The tray of meat was $11 and camping mats were $10. So what does a tray of meat have to do with camping mats? Nothing at all, but it was an opportunity to explain a few concepts relating to money to her.

It also teaches them the concept of value and how to work out priorities when the budget is tight.

Meat is expensive

In addition to health reasons, the cost of meat is one of the reasons why people often limit their meat intake. When the budget is tight, meat is usually the first item to be dropped from the grocery list. Elisabeth has read about war rations and is aware that during World War II, meat dishes were few and far between. The limited supply of meat meant that the price of meat was very high. Now she has a better understanding of why meat dishes were almost non-existent during war times.

Good quality food is expensive

The reason the tray of minced meat cost $11 is because it has a four-star health rating. I could have bought a two-star health rating tray of meat which would have been cheaper, but it wouldn't be as healthy for us. The reason this tray of meat is so expensive depends on the living conditions and diet of the animal. Expensive meat often is the result of better living conditions (free range rather than behind cages) and more natural diets (grass-fed rather than grain-fed) for the animal.

Priorities

In order for us to afford to eat better, we have to make sacrifices elsewhere. I have previously explained to Elisabeth that if we are careful with our money, we can afford to buy good quality items when we need it. We don't spend much on junk food so that we can spend more on good quality food. All of this conversation took place on the way home from the shopping centre – 15 minutes.

> We don't spend much on junk food so that we can spend more on good quality food.

Looking at receipts from different shops also teaches children how to shop around for items they need. When Elisabeth looked at the shopping receipt, she asked whether Aldi was more expensive than Woolworths. Both shops are within five minutes' walk from each other, inside the same shopping centre. I said that Aldi is usually cheaper, but it would depend on what we buy. Sometimes when Woolworths discounts their items, it can work out to be cheaper. That's why we need to know the price of the items so that we know when something is a bargain or a good value.

I sometimes take the children to different shops to show them the differences in pricing. Common staples such as bread and popular breakfast cereals are stocked in all grocery stores, so this is an easy exercise to do. I used to keep a price list for the more common grocery items we buy. I found this to be a fantastic way to know for sure when a bargain came along and be able to stock up with confidence. Asking the children to do this will increase their awareness of the prices of various grocery items. It will teach them the concept of inflation if they see the price of groceries creep up over time. It also teaches them to be aware of clever marketing tactics employed by companies. Many times, we see little to no increase in the price, but the contents of the product has decreased – the packets are getting smaller for the same price.

I used to keep a price list for the more common grocery items we buy.

My children once bought ice creams from the convenience store after school. They thought paying $1 for an icy pole was a good deal, until I showed them a box of eight from Woolworths costing $5 and taught them how to work out unit pricing. In addition to unit pricing, I also explained to them why their icy pole was more expensive at the convenience store – they are paying for the convenience. I explained the mark-up process of a business model. The more intermediaries an item goes through between manufacturing and the final seller, the more incremental costs are added to the item. Small shops aren't necessarily being greedy when they mark up their prices. Rather, they do so to help pay for their own fixed costs such as rental, electricity for the freezer, shop keeper's wages, etc. Small shops also don't have the bargaining power to buy in bulk for a larger discount, so their purchase price may actually be more than the purchase price paid by a much larger grocery store.

I also have a conversation with them about supporting local shops. Even though the prices may be more expensive, it isn't always about the money. Local shops contribute to the community feel of the neighbourhood and it's nice to be able to walk into the shops and be able to greet others by their name and be greeted by our names.

Even though the prices may be more expensive, it isn't always about the money.

2 | Make it real

One of the best ways to teach young children is through games. Teaching children money concepts is no different. However, playing a game with pretend money and playing with real money are two very different experiences.

Board games

I love playing board games with my children. There are a variety of board games tailored to teaching children about money. Modern versions of the board games are usually more colourful, creative and attractive, but I have found the older versions to be the best at teaching money fundamentals. Life was less complicated a few decades ago, there were fewer options to choose from and so it was easier to teach money fundamentals. Today, the availability of resources ought to make teaching money fundamentals easier (if one knows where to look) but the complexity and availability of many options to choose from has made teaching money fundamentals a bit more complicated and overwhelming.

If your children are board game enthusiasts, get them to play the same board game with real money. This was exactly what a father did. For a fun experiment on how children's attitudes change, a father asked his children to play Monopoly using real money. There was a prize for the winner at the end. This experiment was to show the difference between children playing Monopoly with play money and real money. The outcome may surprise you. Check it out on YouTube (https://www.youtube.com/watch?v=_VB39Jo8mAQ).

Games such as *Monopoly*, *Pay Day* and *The Game of Life* have become my family's favourites. After watching the YouTube clip, I am keen to play these games with my children using real money. It will be interesting to see what happens.

> For a fun experiment on how children's attitudes change, a father asked his children to play Monopoly using real money.

Give them a budget

Another opportunity to teach your children about spending wisely is to give them a budget at the next family outing. When you hand over a set amount of money to the children to spend on the outing, be very clear on the rules. Some rules you may wish to have with this 'free' money are:

- You can only spend on food and drinks, not toys.
- Whatever you don't spend you can keep.
- Once it's gone, it's gone. You can't ask me for more.
- It's your decision on what food and drinks you buy. You don't need to ask me for permission nor do you need validation for your decision.

I did this exercise with my children one time we visited the zoo. When we got to the zoo, I told the children they had $10 to spend for the three of them. This money came from selling their unused toys. I made it clear that $10 was all they had and once it's gone, it's gone. My rules were that they can buy themselves a treat, but it cannot be something they bring home at the end of the day (i.e. not toys, souvenirs, other clutter, etc).

Elisabeth proceeded to calculate how much each child was allowed to spend – approximately $3.30. David immediately said he wanted an ice block which costs $2.50. Richard didn't want to spend on anything just yet. After lunch, David said he wanted some popcorn to eat while we watched animal performances. The popcorn was $4.00. Elisabeth was starting to get annoyed and told David he had spent some of his share of the money and therefore didn't have enough money to buy any popcorn. I informed them that I never said they had $3.30 each to spend. They had $10 to spend for the outing and if one child chooses to spend all $10 on himself or herself, then that child will have to contend with the siblings' wrath. David sheepishly asked if Elisabeth and Richard wanted to share some popcorns while watching the animal show. Both siblings agreed.

On the way home, Elisabeth wanted to buy an apple pie. The cost of the apple pie was $2.50. I asked the children to add up how much they had spent. It was $9. I then asked how much each child had spent and Elisabeth and David realised that there isn't much left over for Richard to spend on himself. So they asked Richard what he wanted that was $1 or less. Richard simply said he'd be happy with a soft serve from McDonald's for $0.70. So at the end of the outing, the children had spent $9.70 and had $0.30 left over. Elisabeth announced that Richard hadn't spent much on himself, so it's only fair he keeps the left over money. Richard replied that all he wanted was a soft serve. He got what he wanted, just like everyone else got what they wanted. The fact that his was cheaper didn't matter because not everyone has to spend the same. He gave 10 cents to each of his brother and sister. I was mighty proud of all three children that day.

Pretend shop

Young children like to play pretend shop using real money. When they were younger, my children often lined up their 'stuff' – dolls, cars, trains, books, handmade items, a rock they found outside, anything – and put price tags on them. They then invited the 'public' (i.e. the other members of the family) to come into their shop and buy things. The other children would just pay the price stated on the tag, but I prefer to teach some negotiation skills. I'd usually ask for ridiculously deep discounts on bulk buys. Initially, the shop keeper would reluctantly accept the price offered. I took the opportunity to explain that we don't chase the dollar for the sake of it. If they really believed the value of the item is so much more than the price offered, they can either decline the offer or perhaps make a counter-offer and explain the benefits of the item to convince the customer they are getting a bargain. At the end of this game, we'd return the money to its rightful owner.

I have found the last game particularly useful in setting the children up to run a garage sale. It establishes the mindset that their 'stuff' can in fact bring money. It helps them count money and give back change. It also teaches them a bit of negotiation skills and the ability to explain the value of their items to someone else. If they are struggling to explain the value of their item, this is a good indication that it's junk.

3 | Eat in, then charge for it

Pick a meal that you want to serve restaurant style or café style. Go through the whole motion – set the table up nicely, prepare a main menu, dessert and a choice of drinks. Prepare and serve the meal as someone would in a café or restaurant. After dessert, and after you ask all the 'patrons' how their meal was, present them with a bill. You will get protests and exclamations of unfairness. Amuse yourself as much as you want in this exercise – after all, you're just giving them the opportunity to refine their debating skills.

At the end of the commotion explain to the children the amount on the bill is what it *costs* you to prepare and serve the meal. If they were to eat and drink the same in a restaurant or café, it would cost more because the owner has to charge enough to cover the cost of wages for the chef and waiter, electricity, gas, rent, etc and then add a profit margin on top. The value in this exercise is that it teaches children why eating out is more expensive than eating at home.

I often do this with my children's favourite drinks. Elisabeth likes hot chocolate, Richard likes banana milkshakes and David likes mango smoothies. I'd make these drinks and then ask them to pay for it before they are served the drinks. If I expected protests, I'm never disappointed. Their reaction meant they had learnt something from this exercise. This has definitely made my children become more aware of how much their drinks cost when they buy it from the shops. They also realise that what mum charges them for their large drink is actually a bargain! In short, they have developed an appreciation for mum's cooking. I now get frequent complements from my children about how much nicer my meals taste, compared to what can be bought outside the home.

4 | Look for alternatives

In today's world of abundance, the easy and default response to a problem is to just buy the solution. Growing up, I was told that it is easier to just go out and work to pay for the item we want. This may be an option for adults who earn a high income but it instils a certain attitude and habit in our children which will not serve them well in the future if they don't earn a high income. Worse still, it encourages the mindset of always continuing to work to be able to buy the things they want. It does not encourage creativity in coming up with a solution. These are reasons why I am teaching my children to find alternative ways of satisfying what they want or need, despite it being easier in the short term to buy the solution.

One alternative to buying an item is to make the item. Many grocery items can be made at home. I used to think I need a lot of time to make food from basic staples. However, I have since found out that many of my family's favourite foods can be made with extravagance or they can be made simply. Sometimes we need to have the correct utensils to make it easier for ourselves. For example, a food processor makes it easier and quicker to chop up vegetables.

One alternative to buying an item is to make the item.

Another alternative is to borrow. There are toy libraries where members borrow toys the same way as borrowing books from libraries. If there isn't a toy library near you, ask your children to form one with their friends. See if they can borrow the toys from a friend. Chances are the friend is likely to have played with that toy for a while and would be happy to exchange it with a 'new' toy from your child's toy box. Sharing comes naturally for children. Be sure to tell your children the downsides of lending – the items lent can get dirty, damaged, lost or not returned – so make sure they only lend items where they accept not having the item returned or returned in not as good a condition.

> Hiring items also overcomes the problem of finding space ...

Hiring the item is a third option. DVDs can be hired instead of buying them. Movies and songs can also be downloaded for a fee. If your child doesn't ride the bicycle frequently, it could be an option to hire a bicycle when he wants to go bike riding. I recently found out a shop nearby that hires out bicycles quite cheaply for a few hours or a few days. They also have bicycle trailers for hire. Hiring items also overcomes the problem of finding space to store things in the home. Space is at a premium when we live in a small home!

5 | Children to pay their own

Many parents believe that it is their responsibility to pay for everything their young children want, provided the parents agree with those wants. Parents want to provide a childhood that is as fun and care-free as possible for their children. There is nothing wrong with wanting this for our children and in fact should be encouraged. It becomes a problem when parents associate money as the killjoy to a fun and care-free childhood. Many parents believe that if children are exposed to money transactions, it takes the fun out of their childhood. So parents end up paying for everything in order for their children to truly enjoy their experiences.

For example, if a child has been invited to a birthday party, the parents feel it is their responsibility to buy the friend's birthday present. Similarly if a child goes to the movies, the parents feel they have to buy their child's tickets, popcorn and a drink. If the child is going to the movies with their friend, the parents feel they have to give their children some money to spend. I was brought up this way. My mother would often give me money to spend whenever I went out with my friends or if we were out shopping and I wanted a donut, she'd buy one for me. I wasn't spoilt - these outings were very few and far between and is the reason why my mother paid for these outings. She wanted them to be special for me and she didn't want the lack of money to be a hindrance to my enjoyment.

> Times have changed since I was a child.

The inner-rebel in me is bringing up my children with the opposite attitude. Why? Times have changed since I was a child. The world I grew up in is very different to the one my children are currently growing up. Outings were special for me as a child because we didn't have many of those. The trip to the movies was an exciting adventure and it was a privilege to be invited to a birthday party. My mother simply wanted to make sure I could really enjoy myself on these rare occasions, without having to worry or go without because of the lack of money. When it comes to my children, outings are no longer rare and reserved only for special occasions. We now have frequent family outings and sometimes we may invite the children's friends along. Birthday parties are now occurring more frequently than ever. In the early primary school years, it has become a trend to invite the whole class to birthday parties. The cost of these activities adds up and one way of teaching the children that everything we do has a cost is to show them how much these activities actually cost.

Over time, I have shifted the responsibility of paying for these outings from the parents to the children. I was initially very reluctant to do this because I thought I would dampen my children's enjoyment of these outings. But it hadn't. In fact, knowing how much it costs (and also having to pay) made my children appreciate these outings more.

We recently went to the movies as a family. We chose a cinema that had the cheapest ticket within walking distance from our home. After the movies, I asked them what they thought about the outing. One of my children started to complain the theatre wasn't as nice as the other movie theatres we used to go to, but then added that at least we got to go and watch a movie and it was cheaper than the other theatres, so we had fun but also saved some money.

Paying for junk food, snacks and treats

It is the parent's responsibility to provide food and drinks for their children. However, it's *not* the parent's responsibility to pay for their children's junk food. Snacks and treats are junk food – a packet of chips, a bottle of juice or a can of soft drink.

If our children insist on parents paying for their snacks and treats, then we get to choose what they eat and drink. I often suggested a piece of fruit or home-made muesli bar or home-made muffin. Miraculously my children's hunger disappears when these were their only options.

> ... it's *not* the parent's responsibility to pay for their children's junk food.

One way to encourage children to find alternatives to spending money to satisfy what they want is to ask them to pay for their own junk food, snacks and treats. Previously, when we went to the movies, the smell of popcorn would often entice my children to ask to buy popcorn. It didn't matter they had just had a big meal or that the bucket of popcorn costs ten times as much as one made from home, they just want popcorn to eat while watching a movie. Pestering begins. I started to dread taking the children to the movies. To curb that, I imposed a rule that I will pay for the movie ticket, but anything additional must be paid for by the children. The recent movie outing I described above is an example of how I dealt with the popcorn problem. I reminded my children to bring their money to buy their own popcorn and drink if they want to snack during the movie. They don't *need* a snack (they've just had their dinner) but if they *want* a snack, then they have to pay for it with their own money. None of the children brought their own money. Instead, they raided the pantry cupboard for popcorn, biscuits and drinks to bring to the cinema.

Paying for birthday presents

I was reluctant to write about this, because it is controversial and will not suit many parents. However, if I am to be honest about how I feel about money and stay true to my values, attitudes and beliefs about money, I need to share this family practice.

It works in my family and it was one of the very first lessons I taught my children – many things we do in life involve money. It was also one way to limit the amount of 'disposable income' my children have in the twelve months they are given pocket money.

When I first gave my children pocket money at the age of six years old, the only rule I had was that they had to save half of it. The other half was for them to spend as they pleased. So my children had to save \$3 and have \$3 to spend. Six year olds don't have a lot of things they need, so \$3 is a lot of money for a young child. Six year olds want a lot of things and when they come into contact with a lot of money (for a young child) they tend to go overboard with their spending. My children started to announce that they are rich and that they can buy whatever they want. Whenever we walked past a café, they would want a drink which costs a minimum of $3 these days. But that's okay, because *they* have money to spend. It became a habit that every week they'd ask to go to the café because they have money to spend on their drink.

I wasn't too thrilled with the idea for a few reasons:

- Buying a drink every week is a bad habit. It's full of sugar and besides, making the equivalent at home is much cheaper.
- They don't need it – many adults go for a coffee with friends as an opportunity to meet up or catch up with people. My kids were buying it then drinking on the way home from school. Perhaps it makes them look cool.
- It may be their pocket money, but it came from my hard work. When they spend the pocket money it's like spending my hard work! If I wouldn't have bought them that hot drink with that money, then they shouldn't be buying that stuff.
- I am very careful with my spending and was alarmed by the way they seemed to be so careless with their spending and it was all my doing – I gave them pocket money!

I could have stopped pocket money, but I didn't want to. I was using pocket money to cultivate their habit in saving half of their money. I could have said 'No' to their requests to go to the shops, but that wouldn't be teaching them how to spend their money wisely. They may even get confused about the 'spend half' rule of their pocket money. I could have explained the bad health consequences from consuming too much sugar, but in reality this is often lost on a young child and the lure of a sugary drink is just too much for their impulse and willpower. I could have allowed them to spend their money on the drinks with the consequence that they wouldn't have money left for anything else. This would have taught them wise spending and would have been brilliant, except my children didn't actually have anything else they would spend their money on. It also wouldn't curb the bad habit I was seeing in their spending.

> I decided that I would ask my children to contribute to the cost of their friends' birthday presents.

So I came up with another rule. I made up this rule because at that time my children were attending a lot of birthday parties. It seems the norm to invite the whole class to birthday parties in the early primary school years. With each birthday party they attended, we had to buy presents. I haven't had to buy children's presents for a long time and was shocked to see the prices. So on the one hand, I was spending so much money on birthday presents and my children were being so careless with their 'disposable income'. I decided that I would ask my children to contribute to the cost of their friends' birthday presents. I initially set $10 as the amount my children have to contribute. I figured this is three weeks of their pocket money and if they put aside some money on the fourth week, they'd have enough saved up by the time we have to buy a present. This meant they only had $2 to spend per month and if they really want that $3 hot chocolate after school, they'd have to save up for two months. I'm fine with them consuming that stuff once every two months.

My children knew that if they didn't have enough money saved up, they wouldn't be able to buy a present. So they have three options: (a) turning up at the party without a present; (b) not going to the party; or (c) not spending their pocket money and saving it up for a present. This rule worked really well in my family. There were months when the children didn't spend any of their money because they knew their friends' birthdays were coming up.

Some parents that I have spoken to about this rule were aghast that I'd impose such draconian measures on my children's happiness and friendship. An invitation to a birthday party is part of the social scene and my children will be ostracised if they aren't seen at the parties. Nevertheless, I am still very much in favour of this rule. It teaches my children so many of life's skills and values:

- It teaches the children to be careful with their spending. When money is gone, it's gone.
- It teaches them budgeting – making their money stretch before the next 'payday'.
- They appreciate the true meaning of friendship – it shouldn't come with a cost.
- They appreciate the true meaning of birthday parties – it is a celebration of their special day with people they truly care about and love. It's not about the number of presents they receive. This is also why my children are taught not to expect any presents on their birthday parties. For parents who feel uncomfortable about showing up to parties without a present, we give parents the option to gift second hand pre-loved items (such as books) instead.

They appreciate the true meaning of birthday parties – it is a celebration of their special day with people they truly care about and love.

There were protests from my children when I first introduced this rule. They complained of unfairness, about how their friends don't have to pay for anything and they have to pay for everything. This is a very common reaction and one I am now used to dealing with. No doubt this has set me up for dealing with the same complaints in the future, when my children are teenagers.

This is where every family's values, attitudes and beliefs about spending money will shape what we decide to teach our children. Mine will be different to yours. The important thing is to keep having the conversation with our children about what we do with our money.

Paying for variable costs during a holiday

I have done the same exercise with asking the children to contribute towards the cost of family holidays. In Chapter 6, I gave the example of asking my children to save towards the variable costs of our family holidays. Their saving becomes their spending on family holidays. They decide in advance what activities they want to spend their money on. If they change their mind, while on holiday, and decide not to do that activity, then I return their money for the activity, provided the activities have not been pre-paid.

Asking my children to pay for variable costs of the family holiday has had the effect of teaching them to prioritise their spending.
If there are activities the parents would like their children to try or the parents think may be beneficial to the children, the parents would of course pay for those activities. In one of our skiing trips, we thought it might be a good idea for the children to try their hand (legs?) at snow-boarding. We decided we would pay for their snow-boarding gear and lessons.

A conversation led by the children

I have long held the belief that the best way to teach children in the ages of six through to twelve years of age is by using physical cash. I anticipate that my children will start using other forms of payment – such as debit cards – when they are teenagers. Due to my long-held belief, I hadn't planned on introducing the concept of spending with a credit card to my children until they are at least in the late teenage years (after I have had the talk about debit cards with them). But six year old David had other plans.

> ... I hadn't planned on introducing the concept of spending with a credit card to my children until they are at least in the late teenage years ...

As I became more conscious about having money conversations with my children, I realised that the timing of these conversations isn't always when we plan it to be. It can happen at any time and often it is the children who will initiate the conversation.

Here's a conversation I never expected from a six year old. If you've been following this theme, you will soon realise that I have a lot of unexpected and interesting conversations with my six year old.

> We went to watch *Beauty and the Beast* one evening at the cinema. In the past, we used movie vouchers and didn't really pay much attention to the cost of tickets. This time, we had to pay for the movie tickets and I informed the children how much each ticket costs. My children asked how much the ticket used to cost when we'd go every school holiday. I said the cost was converted from

points, so we didn't really have to pay for the tickets. The older kids were content with the answer but David wanted to know more about where the points came from. I proceeded to explain that the points were accumulated each time we spent money with our credit card. He then asked what a credit card was. I explained to him it's the plastic I have been using to pay for groceries (he's seen me used a credit card many times) and each time I spent money with the card, I accumulated points. When I have sufficient points, I can exchange those points for other things like a movie ticket. He then asked 'So the more we spend, the more points we get?' I confirmed his understanding uneasily and hastened to add that it would be unwise if I simply spent money just to get those points because it would be like spending money to buy those points and then using those points to get whatever I wanted. It is always cheaper to just spend money to buy the things I wanted instead of buying those things through points. It is wiser to use the credit card to pay for things we needed to pay for – such as groceries, electricity, gas and water bills, school fees, etc and in that process, accumulate the points. This, I reasoned is because we have to spend the money anyway and getting points is simply an added bonus. It would be unwise if we bought unnecessary things just to get those points.

A few weeks later, I took all three children grocery shopping with me. At the check-out, I pulled out my credit card, gave it to Richard (then nine years old) and asked him to tap on the PayWave. He handed the credit card back to me and I casually commented, 'Isn't it awesome that I just paid for the groceries without any money?' Richard laughed and replied, 'No, a credit card is using money.' I queried, 'But it's free money, isn't it? I just use the card and you didn't see me using any notes or coins.' Richard was amused and replied, 'You still have to pay it back when the credit card bill comes.' I turned to another child, 'What do you think, David? You agree it's free money, right?' David sighed and replied, 'I don't know.' So a mental note to self – Richard understands credit card and is ready for more complex money lessons. David is still unsure about credit card and I will have to find another opportunity to teach him about credit cards, perhaps when he's a bit older. Elisabeth didn't comment, so I need to ask her another time to gauge her understanding.

Summary

Making unwise spending decisions is the reason many people do not become financially comfortable. Wisdom comes with experience and experience comes with making unwise decisions. It is better to allow our young children to make unwise decisions with their money now when the stakes are not as high than to have them make those same unwise decisions later on when those decisions are more costly. Once they know about what not to do they should learn about what to do, and hence learn about both.

'A fool and his money are soon parted.'
~ Dr John Bridges

Chapter 9
CONCLUSION

Most babies learn to crawl before they can walk and then run. Toddlers learning to walk do so with baby steps before taking bigger strides and finally learning how to run. Children learning to read first learn to recognise the letters of the alphabet and then the sounds of the letters before finally being taught how to read. Children learning arithmetic first learn to recognise numbers. These baby steps create a child's foundation to enable the child to learn more complex skills in life.

It is the same with financial literacy. Young children need to learn basic money skills to create their foundation. Successfully teaching our children to manage money responsibly in the complex world of finance later involves teaching them money baby steps now: earning money, saving money and spending money wisely. Until a child has a firm understanding of these concepts and has cultivated good money habits around these three money concepts, she is not yet ready to learn more complex finance lessons, such as investing, advanced budgeting and managing money generally.

The baby steps that our children take in these early years cultivates their good money habits. It takes an average of 66 days for a new behaviour to become a habit. If our children take one baby step a day, they will have cultivated at least five good money habits by the end of the year. If they take two baby steps a day, they will have cultivated 10 good money habits by the end of the year. The more baby steps they take every day, the more good money habits they will cultivate in a year.

The rate of progression and the lessons taught in each topic depends on the child's financial maturity and understanding rather than her calendar age. Having frequent money conversations is the key to ensuring our children are always learning and refining their financial literacy. These frequent money conversations are the opportunities we present to our children to take their baby steps. Each baby step our children take is then an opportunity to have more money conversations.

How many baby steps will you encourage your children to take today?

Appendix

Opportunities to have money conversations exist everyday and in everything that we do. The more we practise having money conversations with our children, the better we become at identifying these opportunities.

To help you get started, I have listed 10 questions you can ask your children and 10 concepts you can tell your children for each money concept building block.

Money conversations: Earning money

ASK **Questions to ask your children**		**TELL** **Concepts to tell the children**
1	Why do mum and/or dad go to work?	Tell your children the different ways other children have earned money (e.g., selling lemonade, jewellery, etc).
2	What does earning money mean?	Explain to your children why you pay or don't pay them for doing chores.
3	What do you love doing? Can you think of how you can earn money doing what you love?	Talk about pocket money. Explain why you give or not give them pocket money.
4	Is it easy or difficult to earn money? Why?	Tell them one thing that you do to earn money.
5	How do you feel about children being paid to do chores around the home?	Praise your children for one earning money habit they are cultivating.

ASK **Questions to ask your children**		**TELL** **Concepts to tell the children**
6	Why do we need to earn money?	Tell them about your first money-earning activity.
7	What work do people do to earn money? (Expect answers such as teachers and people in other professional jobs.)	Talk about the idea of a garage sale. Then either plan to hold a garage sale or visit one.
8	Pick a task that you do around the home. Ask: are there people who do the same task for money? (e.g. cleaning the home)	Explain the concept of earning: the exchange of time, skills and efforts for money.
9	Do you want to earn money? Why?	Identify the cost of your children's favourite junk food. Work out the hours of work they have to do to earn enough to pay for that item.
10	Why do some people work for free?	Explain why some people are paid more for doing the same work (e.g., teenage babysitters are paid less than professional adult babysitters).

Money conversations: Saving money

ASK Questions to ask your children		TELL Information to tell the children
1	List one thing we did today that saved us money.	Help your children decide on a short-term saving goal.
2	What does saving money mean?	Help your children decide on a medium-term saving goal.
3	What are you saving up towards?	Tell your children about your long-term saving goal.
4	What can we do over the next seven days to save money?	Talk about your children's savings progress visual chart.
5	Where do you keep the money that you're saving?	Discuss the difference between saving and hoarding.
6	What is the purpose of a bank?	Start a family saving bottle.
7	How do you feel about your progress towards your savings goal?	Tell your children about one item you are saving up for.
8	Where do you get money from (e.g. birthday, tooth fairy, etc)?	Praise your children for one saving money habit they are cultivating.
9	Why do you need to save some of your money each time you are given money?	Explain the two aspects of saving money – putting money aside and reducing spending.
10	How do you keep yourself motivated to continue saving when you feel like giving up?	Pick one item you usually buy which you will not buy for the next seven days. Tell your children about it and tell them to keep you accountable.

Money conversations: Spending money

	ASK Questions to ask your children	TELL Information to tell the children
1	Look at a catalogue together. Point out the items that are discounted. Explain how you know this item is discounted. Ask: can you find another item that is discounted?	Make a list of items you want. Show your children the list and explain why you can't have everything you want.
2	Look at a catalogue together. Work out the unit price of one item. Ask: can you work out the unit price of another item?	Pick an extra-curricular activity that your children are engaged in. Tell them how much it costs each time they undertake that activity.
3	Show your children a recent grocery list. Ask: can you put these items into 'needs' and 'wants'.	Show your children the latest utility bill. Explain how much it costs to use the utility and how the cost is calculated.
4	Is spending money a good thing or a bad thing? Why?	Explain comparison pricing.
5	What is the difference between an item we want and an item we need?	Give an example of a wise spending decision. Explain why it was wise.
6	How much did our meal cost today?	Tell the children what you spent your money on today.
7	Pick an advertisement you saw today. What do you think is the message in the advertisement?	Praise your children for one spending money habit they are cultivating.
8	Is your school uniform a 'need' or a 'want'? Why?	Talk about the next family outing. Explain how you will spend money on the next outing.

ASK Questions to ask your children		TELL Information to tell the children
9	What did we spend money on today?	Set a budget for the next grocery trip. Compare budget with actual spend.
10	Show children the receipt from a recent shopping trip. Ask: can you tell me how much I spent on the recent trip to the grocery store?	Work out cost of one glass of milk. Tell your children a babycino from the café costs 50 cents – it's only frothy milk!

Money conversations: General concepts

ASK Questions to ask your children		TELL Information to tell the children
1	What money conversations do you want to have today?	Talk about a board game you've played recently. Introduce the idea of a money board game.
2	What does being rich mean?	Explain the difference between a natural saver vs natural spender.
3	What would you do if you were given $100,000?	Tell your children why you want to teach them about money.
4	How do you know when someone is rich?	Identify one thing that you are grateful for.
5	Do you think we are rich? Why?	Tell your children the importance of having frequent money conversations.
6	Pick out random items around the home. Ask: guess the cost of each item.	Tell your children whether you think you're a natural spender or a natural saver.
7	What do you think will happen if you make mistakes with your money?	Explain the origins of money.
8	Do you think children should learn about money? Why?	Talk about the ideas from a money book written for children.
9	Do you like to spend money or save money? Why?	Tell your children what you think money should be used for.
10	Do you think we need money? Why?	Tell your children why you think money is important.

References

Much of what is written in this book is my original thought. It is my conclusion based on the materials that I have read, trial and error within my family, discussions with family and friends and my own thought process. However, in writing this book, I referred to the following resources:

1. ASIC's Money Smart Website (www.moneysmart.gov.au).
2. Sharon Beder with Wendy Varney and Richard Gosden, This Little Kiddy Went to Market: The Corporate Capture of Childhood, Pluto Press, London, 2009.
3. Ron Lieber, The Opposite of Spoiled: Raising Kids Who Are Grounded, Generous and Smart About Money, HarperCollins Publishers, New York, 2015.
4. Bonnie Worth, One Cent, Two Cents, Old Cent, New Cent: All About Money, Random House Children's Books, New York, 2008.
5. Dave Ramsey and Rachel Cruze, Smart Money Smart Kids: Raising the Next Generation to Win with Money, Lampo Press, Tennessee, 2014.

On a more general level, my values, attitudes and beliefs about money and life are shaped by my life experiences, podcasts I listen to as well as books that I read. Recent books that have continued to influence my thinking and my writing include:

1. Brene Brown, The Gifts of Imperfection, Hazelden Publishing, Minnesota, 2010.
2. Brene Brown, Daring Greatly, Penguin Life, 2013.
3. Brene Brown, Rising Strong, Vermilion, London, 2015.
4. Vicki Robin and Joe Dominguez, Your Money or Your Life, Penguin Books, London, 2008.
5. Thomas J. Stanley and William D. Danko, The Millionaire Next Door, Harper Business, Sydney, 1996.
6. Thomas J. Stanley, Millionaire Women Next Door, Andrews McMeel Publishing, Missouri, 2004.
7. Carol S. Dweck, Mindset, Ballantine Books, New York, 2006.

About

Amy Koit is first and foremost a mother to three young children, Elisabeth, Richard and David. She lives in Sydney, Australia with her children and husband, Alaric. Amy became more intentional in teaching her children about money when her eldest child, Elisabeth, was six years old. For many years, she has researched various ways to teach children about money and has tried many of these methods on her children. Amy's system involves cultivating good money habits, and is one that all parents can use to teach their own children about money. Her system has led to a transformation in the way her children perceive and use money. This provides a good basis for them to managing money.

Amy is a lawyer with LLB (Hons) and B.Com degrees from the University of Queensland and a Master in Taxation from the University of New South Wales. She is a solicitor of the Supreme Court of NSW and a Fellow at The Tax Institute of Australia. Amy is also a Chartered Accountant and is a member of the Chartered Accountants Australia and New Zealand.

Amy has a passion for teaching, having taught at various universities including the University of Sydney and the University of NSW. She has received five Dean's Citations for Teaching over two years at the University of Sydney, where she teaches law to postgraduate students.

Having heard so many parents comment that "more should be done about children's financial literacy" but many not knowing what ought to be done, she decided to use her passion for teaching to focus on helping parents become intentional in teaching their children about money.

You can read more about Amy's thoughts and ideas on Kids Money Habits (www.kidsmoneyhabits.com). It is where she shares many of her thoughts and ideas on how she is cultivating good money habits in her children every day.

Index

D

E

F

G

H

I

J

K

L

M

N

O

P

R

S

Made in the USA
Monee, IL
08 November 2026

68020207R00146